MW00423830

THE
MILLION-DOLLAR FINANCIAL ADVISOR TEAM

THE

THE
MILLION-DOLLAR
FINANCIAL
ADVISOR
TEAM

Best Practices from Top-Performing Teams

DAVID J. MULLEN JR.

HARPERCOLLINS
LEADERSHIP

AN IMPRINT OF HARPERCOLLINS

Published by HarperCollins Leadership, an imprint of HarperCollins.

Book design by Elyse Strongin, Neuwirth & Associates.

ISBN 978-0-8144-3921-0 (eBook)

Library of Congress Cataloging-in-Publication Data

Names: Mullen, David J., Jr., author.
Title: The million-dollar financial advisor team : best practices from top performing teams / by David J. Mullen, Jr.
Description: New York : AMACOM Logo, [2018] | Includes index.
Identifiers: LCCN 2018005008 (print) | LCCN 2018012088 (ebook) | ISBN 9780814439210 (ebook) | ISBN 9780814439203 (hardcover)
Subjects: LCSH: Financial planners. | Financial services industry. | Business communication. | Teams in the workplace.
Classification: LCC HG179.5 (ebook) | LCC HG179.5 .M855 2018 (print) | DDC 332.6068/4–dc23
LC record available at https://lccn.loc.gov/2018005008

ISBN 978-0-8144-3920-3

Printed in the United States of America
18 19 20 21 22 LSC 10 9 8 7 6 5 4 3 2 1

To my loving family, who have always provided uncondi-
tional love and support. Thank you, Cynthia, Nathan, David,
John, and Katie. And to my parents, the late David Sr. and
Rosemary Mullen; not only were they wonderful parents
but they were both teachers who inspired in me the joy of
sharing knowledge with others.

Acknowledgments

I would like to thank the members of the Altius Learning Team who lent their expertise, experience, and support in the writing of this book—thank you, Carl Meyer, Frank Beyer, Peter DiCenso, Alane Siem, and Bobby Theriot. I want to especially thank my partner at Altius, Jim Dullanty, for his many contributions, in particular for his work on the world-class offering chapter.

I would also like to thank the partners on the highly functioning teams that I interviewed. They were all extremely generous with their time. These top advisors openly shared their extraordinary team best practices, unselfishly giving me their time so that my readers could benefit from their knowledge and experience.

I would also like to thank Dr. Richard Orlando and Tim McManus for the invaluable insights that were most helpful in creating the leadership chapter.

Lastly, I would also like to thank the publishing team, beginning with my agent Welly Keller, and HarperCollins Leadership for believing in this book. Pam Liflander has been my editing partner, providing her expertise to make the most of my work.

Contents

THE
MILLION-DOLLAR FINANCIAL ADVISOR TEAM

Introduction

The number of teams in the financial services industry has exploded. The evolution of teams started slowly in the 1990s. Before then, the vast majority of financial advisors were sole practitioners. Gradually the formation of teams began to gain traction, and by the early 2000s advisory teams exploded. Today the majority of financial advisors are either part of a team or would like to be on a team. Many experts predict that by 2020, 80 percent of all financial advisors will be on a team.

There is no question in most financial advisors' minds that they would be more productive being on a team compared to working as a sole practitioner. However, despite the research and all the reasons why advisors on teams are more productive, not all advisors find their way onto a team, and not all teams are highly functioning. In fact, many function at a low level, causing the advisors to have lower productivity than they had as sole practitioners.

This book will show advisors who are currently not on a team how to build one or join one. More importantly, this book is meant to help create successful, highly functioning teams. It is designed to provide guidelines and tactics for financial advisory teams to reach their full potential through "team best practices."

MY STORY

In 1980, I started my career as a financial advisor at Merrill Lynch as a sole practitioner. Over the next two years, I built a good foundation for my practice and consistently ranked in the top quintiles of financial advisors that had the same experience level. In 1982, my good friend Bob Wolter—who was also a financial advisor in my office—approached me about partnering together and forming a team. Even though teaming was not a common practice in 1982, the idea made sense and appealed to me. However, there were no other teams in our office or our region. For that matter, I had only heard of a few teams at Merrill Lynch as a company. Our manager was skeptical but didn't want to stand in the way of two successful advisors who were highly motivated to grow their business.

Being part of a team for the next three years propelled my practice to levels I could never have achieved on my own. My partner and I were pioneers—with no guidance, no internal resources, and no books on how to build a successful team. However, what we did have was a very strong motivation to grow, to trust in one another, and to keep an open mind about how to operate together. Without realizing it, my partner and I had developed team best practices that formed the core principles of a highly functioning team. These were based on five early decisions.

Our first big decision was to set short- and long-term goals, and to develop a plan to reach those goals. The second important decision was to meet weekly to discuss the business and where we were each focusing. We realized the importance of communication and having someone else to brainstorm with. I always felt as a sole practitioner that it was "lonely in my own brain," so having a respected colleague who had the same goals for growth to share ideas with was priceless. We would spend hours on Saturdays talking about our goals and developing and refining plans on how to reach them.

Our third decision was to pool our resources and invest back into our business. We invested in an Apple 2E computer (that cost $1,395 in 1983 dollars, almost $15,000 today) to organize our client contact and prospecting efforts. We negotiated with our manager to assign one sales assistant to our team, and we would pay a portion of her salary.

Our fourth decision was to assign specific roles to each of us. I was responsible for prospecting, and Bob was responsible for our investment strategy and portfolio construction. We shared responsibility for client contact. By sharing the day-to-day activities, we were able to be more productive and efficient.

Our fifth decision was to hold each other accountable for our activities and results. We kept track of the number of client and prospect contacts and appointments, as well as new clients brought in and business generated. We reviewed our results during our weekly team meeting—recognizing our individual successes and providing additional motivation to perform our responsibilities by being accountable to each other.

Three years later Bob and I were encouraged to assume managerial positions, and our team dissolved. I was promoted to be an office manager. For the next thirty-five years I would work with many of the industry's highest-functioning teams as a manager and professional coach.

Interestingly, I would see these same team best practices being implemented over and over again. The team best practices that I had discovered myself have been expanded and refined, but the same core principles that served my team so well thirty-seven years ago have continued to be the foundation from which highly functioning teams have been built and maintained.

HOW THIS BOOK WORKS

This book is designed to be a guide for teams to function at the highest levels. The difference between a highly functional and a low-functioning team is incorporating the team best practices. This book was designed to be the bridge between where your team is now and reaching your full potential as a member of a highly functioning team.

My research and observations as a manager and professional coach working with hundreds of teams, many of the most highly functioning in our industry have helped me form the team best practices. I have created them from interviewing highly functioning financial advisory teams that I knew were among the best in the industry. These were teams that I had worked with in the past and that I knew firsthand functioned at the highest level. In all cases the teams had been together for a significant period of time and had continued to grow at an exceptional rate. The team revenue ranged from $2 million to $18 million and in many cases ranked as the most productive and highest producing teams in their firms. They were located throughout the country, on both coasts, in the southeast, midwest, and Rocky Mountain regions. They represent multiple firms and include wire houses, regionals, and independents.

Extensive interviews were conducted with the team leaders and multiple team members. The intent of the interviews was to gain a deep understanding and insight into how their team functioned, how they were organized, and what contributed to their ability to function at such a high level for a sustained period of time. I asked deep, probing questions about their best practices, trends they saw for the future, and mistakes they had learned from. These teams also shared many great anecdotes which I've included in the book. You can learn from real "boots on the ground" experiences of these teams and see how closely they mirror what you may be going through today.

MEET THE TEAMS WITH THE BEST PRACTICES

I selected ten teams from the hundreds I had worked with and interviewed that I featured in the case studies chapter at the end of the book; other team anecdotes are featured in each chapter. While by coincidence, all of the senior partners in the teams I interviewed are male, there are certainly many financial advisor teams with female senior partners and all of the teams in the book have both male and female members.

1. Richard's team consists of four advisors (including himself) and three client associates. Of the four advisors, three have the traditional roles of financial advisors and one is a chief investment manager who has a CFA. They have a total of 150 client relationships that generate approximately $5 million in production.

2. Mike is the senior partner of his team, which includes four other members. There is one client associate who is the chief operating officer of the team as well as three financial analysts—two of whom are CFAs while the other is working on getting his CFA. Mike's team generates $6 million in production.

3. Harold is a senior partner and formed a team with six other partners with experience levels from seven to forty years. They also have three investment associates who have specific focuses: a 401k specialist, a fixed income specialist, and a relationship manager (assigned smaller accounts). The team also has a chief investment analyst and two assistants that support him. In addition, the team has four senior client associates who are responsible for servicing the team's clients and are each assigned to one or two of the team's partners. The team also has two junior client associates who support the senior client associates and two junior financial advisors who have not yet earned partner status—which is dependent on their ability to bring in new assets. (They are the sons of the team's founding partners.) Currently the team generates $18 million in production and is the largest producing team in their region.

4. Charles and Steve run a horizontal team: They are the two senior partners. They also have three client associates, an analyst, and a junior partner responsible for planning and next-generation clients. The team produces $8 million.

5. Jim's team started as a vertical team but has evolved into a horizontal team as his son Jim Jr. has gained the experience to be

a senior partner. There are currently four FA team members, two senior client associates, and one junior client associate. The team does $5 million on $1.1 billion in assets and has a total of 300 relationships.

6. Ken runs a vertical team with his junior partner Mike. Mike is considerably younger than Ken and is an important part of Ken's long-term succession plan. The team is doing $3 million in business, on $330 million in assets. The team has two senior client associates: Chris has worked with Ken for twenty-two years, and Kate has been on the team for thirteen years. The team also has a junior client associate who works part time.

7. Henry runs a vertical team with all of the business going through Henry's production number and has junior partner Tom compensated as an employee. They have one senior client associate who has worked with them for over ten years. The team currently works with 85 core client relationships and manages $275 million in assets, while producing $2 million in business.

8. John runs a vertical team and is the sole equity partner. He has a junior partner and an investment strategist who is also the relationship manager for several of the team's clients. The team also has an analyst responsible for the portfolio management and a junior analyst that supports him. They have five client managers who are responsible for the servicing of assigned clients, and two junior client associates who support them. In addition, they have a full-time team manager who is John's chief of staff and handles the day-to-day oversight of the team operations. John's team does $15 million in production and is the third-highest producer with one of the largest financial services firms in the industry.

9. Nelson runs a vertical team with two junior partners. Nelson looks at his team as a franchise opportunity and has encouraged

other financial advisors to join his team. In addition to the three core partners the team has added five other partners who fit the franchise model. The franchise team members have the benefit of being part of a $15 million team that's ranked by *Barron's* and a Fortune Top 400 financial advisory team. The team also has four relationship managers, five administrative managers, and two wealth management strategists. Nelson's executive assistant doubles as the team's operations manager.

10. Paul believes that the structure of a law firm fits very well in a financial service practice and has organized his team using that structure. The team has a hierarchy of senior partners, junior partners, client relationship managers, and client associates. This team is a horizontal model with two senior partners, five client relationship managers, and also three client associates. Paul's team does $4.5 million in business with assets under management of $620 million.

THE TEAM BEST PRACTICES

Inside this book, you will learn how each of the best practices is used efficiently, and you'll learn from the anecdotal experience of the teams. Not every team worked exactly the same way, or had the same number of members, but all of them in one way or another maintained these best practices:

- **Establishing a Vision.** The best teams develop a vision of where they want their team to be and what they want it to look like in the future. They have a relentless commitment to improve and work toward reaching their full potential. They understand that the entire team functions at a higher level when the team members are inspired by this vision of what the team can become, and they communicate that vision on every possible occasion.

The highest-functioning teams also recognize that having and sharing a vision is not enough; they also must develop a business plan to achieve their vision. A vision without a plan is a dream; a vision with a plan turns the dream into a reality. You will see how this business plan is the equivalent of the blueprint or architectural design for building a dream house.

- **Roles and Responsibilities.** The highest-functioning teams understand that a team does best when each member has clearly defined roles and responsibilities. Clear job descriptions are critical. Without clear roles and responsibilities, individual team members can't be held accountable for their performance, and compensation becomes a murky issue.

- **Performance Measurements.** The best teams understand that roles and responsibilities must have measurable outcomes. Each member needs to be assigned activities and goals that relate to clear performance measurements and subsequent reviews. When individuals have clarity about what is expected of them through objective measurements and are held accountable to those expectations through periodic reviews, their performance will improve.

- **Compensation.** The highest-functioning teams realize that they need to retain their best team members through fair and generous compensation. A team always functions better when the most productive team members are retained. These loyal team members create an environment of stability, high performance, and good morale. Compensation schemes that tie roles and responsibilities to measurable activities and goals and regular performance reviews produce the best results for both the individual and the team.

- **Communication.** Frequent and consistent communication is a characteristic that the highest-functioning teams embrace. Team communication reinforces the team vision as well as the progress toward the team goals. Additionally, team communication provides a venue for team members to brainstorm and share ideas on how to better function in the future and provides a venue for accountability.

- **Hiring.** The best teams understand that their team is only as good as the sum of its parts. They take hiring new team members very seriously and have a thoughtful and thorough hiring process. The best teams are also clear on their hiring needs, including what additional roles will be needed as the team grows. Additionally, they understand that developing a training program for new hires is just as important as retention.

- **The Product: A World-Class Offering.** A team is only as good as the offering that it provides its clients and prospective clients. The highest-functioning teams have committed to develop and implement a wealth management offering that adds consistent value to their clients and allows them to charge a premium. Their offering is part of the DNA of the team and each team member understands their roles in delivering at the highest levels. This offering must be articulated to their clients and prospective clients through their value proposition.

- **Marketing.** The highest-functioning teams are acutely focused on the acquisition of new clients and assets. Just like any successful business in any industry, these teams have a marketing division. Its purpose is to have proactive marketing processes designed to grow their team's practice.

- **Processes.** The highest-functioning teams all have a process-based practice. They understand the more processes they have, the more efficient and productive they are, and the more scalable their practice becomes. These teams have established a process for every aspect of their practice, including their wealth management offerings, client services, administration, and marketing. Chapter 11 includes a process gap analysis tool that can help you evaluate existing processes as well as identify needed processes. Team processes need to be reviewed periodically to evaluate their effectiveness.

- **Leadership.** The best teams have strong and consistent leadership. The team leaders embrace and execute essential leadership principles that motivate, retain, and bring out the best work and commitment among team members. You will learn that seniority is not necessarily the first consideration for selecting a team leader. I have seen many instances when a junior team member can be more qualified to be a team leader than the most senior partner.

LET'S GET STARTED

Our industry has changed dramatically over the thirty-seven years since I started as a new advisor in 1980, and in almost all ways for the better. The role of a financial advisor has evolved from a "sales person—account executive" to a trusted advisor. Today's advisor is not focused on the sale but rather on providing financial advice with the objective of guiding clients to reaching their financial goals. Being on a team is more client centric and enables FAs to do their jobs better and be more productive. Let's start by understanding why the best teams are formed.

1

The Case for Teams

One of the best descriptions of a team that I have seen is from Jon Katzenbach, an organizational consultant, who describes a team in the following way: "A small number of people with complementary skills who are committed to a common purpose, performance goals, and approach for which they hold themselves mutually accountable."

Teams are the future of financial services, and experts have repeatedly shown that advisors working on teams outperform sole practitioners. Recently there was an extensive study done by PriceMetrix that quantified the value of teams. In this study, the researchers found that teams have a higher propensity to do the right things that cause their business to grow. The study also found that the increased accountability of working on a team promoted a higher level of discipline in individual team members. The Price-Metrix study also showed that teams have 17 percent more assets than sole practitioners. In fact, clients have shown a greater willingness to consolidate their assets with a team. Teams retained their most affluent clients longer and had clients with more assets. The study also revealed that productivity was higher for advisors on teams, with assets growing at an 11 percent higher rate and revenue 17 percent higher.

My own observations of working with many of the top teams in our industry is that for an advisor who aspires to reach a million- and ultimately a multimillion-dollar practice, being on a team is essential for the following reasons:

- **Accountability.** Financial advisors, like everyone else, perform better when they are accountable to someone. A highly functioning team has accountability through clearly defined roles and responsibilities, performance reviews, and compensation. This level of accountability is not possible for a sole practitioner.

- **Idea Sharing.** Financial advisors who work together to achieve common team goals are able to strategize and share ideas on how to improve their practices. This extends to marketing, portfolio management, client service, and improved team processes.

- **Resources.** Pooling resources together to invest back into the team has significant and positive ramifications for team growth. Having more money to invest in administrative members, marketing budgets, and client service increases productivity.

- **Client Driven.** All the research I have seen and my own experience validate that clients prefer working with a team as opposed to a sole practitioner. The primary reasons are a transparent succession plan, better service, and more depth of expertise. The more satisfied the clients, the more assets, more referrals, more business, and higher retention the team will get from each highly satisfied client.

- **Succession Planning.** This allows the individual clients to feel confident of the continuity of their relationship with the team. It also provides peace of mind to the advisors that their clients will be taken care of when they exit from the business, as well as creating enterprise value upon retirement for the partners.

- **Increased Capacity and Delegation.** Having multiple team members with different responsibilities enables each individual team member to specialize and focus more on their primary areas of expertise. Individual FAs can focus and spend more time with fewer, more affluent clients. They have more time to prospect because of the increased capacity. Delegation enables financial advisors to spend much more of their time on what I call the big three: developing and implementing their wealth management offering, contacting their best clients, and prospecting new affluent clients.

- **Client Communication.** One of the great values of a team is the positive impact on perception that it has for the team's clients. Clients consider it a benefit when they know what's going on with their advisor's team: knowing there is a succession plan in place, and that when their financial advisor is away from the office they are still covered. Introducing the new team and sharing the benefits should be among the highest priorities a newly formed team has and should be one of the first things to do as the team is formed.

TYPICAL TEAM CHALLENGES

One of the most powerful forces that drives teams to perform at a high level is synergy, the interaction of two or more entities to produce a combined effect greater than the sum of their parts. A synergistic relationship between team members occurs when they brainstorm over ideas to improve their practice, hold each other accountable, have a division of labor where they contribute their different talents to overall functioning of the team, pool financial resources so they can attract and retain high-quality employees, and back each other up when one of the partners is out of the office.

A team of financial advisors is one of the best examples of synergy: When two or more advisors come together they are more productive than they are individually. This powerful force of synergy is what is responsible for highly functioning teams to perform at such a high level.

However, the force of synergy can be reversed with a dysfunctional team. A lack of synergy creates chaos, confusion, infighting, and lower productivity. This occurs largely because of the emotional impact and time wasted on dealing with issues that cause a team to be dysfunctional. Think of a dysfunctional marriage.

The two most common causes of reverse synergy:

1. **Poor planning when forming a team.** Unfortunately, one of the negative impacts of the evolution and proliferation of teams is that teams have been hastily formed without proper due diligence prior to the team's formation. So many advisors feel they are missing out by not being on a team that they form a team just for the sake of being on a team. In my experience, there are too many teams that are functioning at low levels because not enough time was spent during the formation stage of team building. In many ways teams are like a professional marriage, and while no one would argue that a good marriage is always blissful, a bad marriage is miserable. We know that 50 percent of marriages fail as a result of being dysfunctional, and I believe the same is true with financial advisory teams.

2. **Lack of alignment in personal values.** One of the biggest causes of a dysfunctional team is that individual team members' professional and personal values are not aligned. Just as most individuals that can maintain a long-term successful marriage would attribute that success to shared values, the same is true for a financial advisor team. Examples of shared professional values include investment philosophy, commitment to professional development, the wealth-management process, long-term goals, work ethic, service commitment, retained earnings vs. money reinvested back in the business, target clients, infrastructure of the practice, ethics, and trust.

The top advisor teams all have these common shared values. Personal values that should be evident include:

1. Putting the team ahead of individual needs
2. Committing to always doing the right thing for clients and team members
3. Recognizing all members of the team
4. Overcompensating high performing and loyal team members
5. Being client-focused

THE NEXT STEP

Having been part of a team and having worked with countless teams as a manager and professional coach and trainer, I can say without a doubt that teaming makes sense and *every* advisor should strongly consider forming or joining a team. In the next chapter, you'll learn what the secret sauce is for creating a highly functioning team.

2

Forming a
High-Functioning Team

Being part of a high-functioning team is preferable to being a sole practitioner, yet a poorly functioning team can yield the opposite effect. The make or break of a team's success is making sure it includes the right people. In so many ways it's like a professional marriage—the institution of marriage has stood the test of time and very few will argue the benefits of a good marriage. However, the key to a good marriage is who you marry; being in a bad marriage is worse than not being married at all.

Once you make the people decision you can determine the right structure. The structure will drive the right implementation of building a highly functioning team. When I think of my own experience in forming a team, the most important factor was the character and the values of my future partner. I trusted him, I admired his worth ethic, his ambitions were aligned, I liked him, and I respected him. All the other reasons for forming a team were present and have been described in detail, but without the right person none of those other benefits mattered.

UNDERSTANDING THE DIFFERENCES IN TEAM STRUCTURES

With the right people and in the proper situation, any one of a variety of team designs can be very effective. Vertical teams keep things simple and allow the financial advisor to keep control and guide the direction of the team. Horizontal teams can create great synergy yet may develop leadership issues. Alliance teams are easy to put together and allow for team independence but must work hard at resolving issues related to shared resources. Holistic teams offer total solutions and, although more complicated in structure, generally have the most comprehensive product and service offerings.

Vertical Team

A vertical team is designed around a single financial advisor. Typically, this financial advisor is already very successful and wants to build a team to support her strengths so that she can delegate all other responsibilities to other members. One of the biggest benefits of a vertical team is that the financial advisor gets a large majority (typically 80 to 100 percent) of the equity ownership. However, a vertical team will not be able to take full advantage of the brainstorming, succession planning, and specialization features other team structures enjoy.

One of the best examples of a successful vertical team was run by my friend Taylor Glover. Taylor had incredible talent in business development and the ability to develop deep and strong relationships with his best clients. Recognizing his talents, he realized that the best way to capitalize on them was to build a team to support him. He already had a very good client associate but knew he needed more support. He needed a team member who could manage his practice, and he found Art. While Taylor was involved and provided oversight, Art ran the day-to-day business for the team. Art was not the rainmaker that Taylor was, and didn't have the deep relationships with Taylor's best clients, but he was highly organized, had strong interpersonal and communication skills, and had experience running a business. Art took over the responsibility for managing the team. He developed a superior service model, managed the other team members, ensured the investment strategy and models were implemented, and acted as the relationship manager for many of Taylor's clients.

After a few years, Taylor added Austin as another relationship manager, while Art continued to manage and add client associates and team administrative managers as needed. Over the fifteen-year period that Taylor and Art worked together, the practice tripled to

$14 million, and Taylor was Merrill Lynch's largest producer at the time. While Taylor kept 100 percent of the equity ownership, he paid Art extremely well. When Taylor retired, Art become the largest equity partner of the team and has since led the team to even greater success.

The potential roles on a vertical team include:

- **Partner.** Holds majority equity ownership
- **Financial Planner or Investment Associate.** Oversees the planning process for the team's best clients
- **Financial Analyst.** Oversees the investment process and investment strategy
- **Relationship Manager(s).** Oversees assigned, smaller relationships
- **Team Manager.** A relationship manager or a junior partner who is responsible for managing the team
- **Administrative Manager(s).** Responsible for the administrative and operational duties of the team and servicing the team's clients

PROS AND CONS OF A VERTICAL STRUCTURE

Positives

➤ Less complex and easier to manage

➤ Minimal conflicts and misunderstandings

➤ Clear leadership

➤ Minimal compensation issues

Negatives

➤ Lack of opportunity to brainstorm and share ideas

➤ Challenge of succession planning

➤ Limited specialization

➤ Challenge of having client coverage when the partner is unavailable

Horizontal Team

This structure is best suited for financial advisors that appreciate the value of collaboration, feedback, brainstorming, and shared decisionmaking. I believe there is merit to the expression "two heads are better than one." I also believe one of the real benefits of a team is to have the opportunity to share ideas, get feedback, get input on decisions, and share accountability—and that these benefits can only be provided by committed and equal team partners. Partners can have different skillsets, areas of expertise, and experiences that can complement one another and expand the reach of the team.

Not all horizontal teams have equal splits, but no single partner has an overwhelming equity position. Each partner's value might not just be the production she generates, but the value she brings through portfolio management or other roles and responsibilities. What's more, a horizontal team only makes sense financially when each team member brings significant value to the team, providing the critical synergy that all high-functioning teams possess. The best horizontal teams have members who strive to contribute more than their equity split. Imagine two team members who are fifty-fifty partners each striving to contribute at a 60 percent level. This level of commitment is essential for the team to do very well and for each partner to be financially successful independently. Otherwise they would be better off in a vertical partnership.

One of the best examples of leading a horizontal team is Ross and Matt. Ross started the practice and built it to close to a million-dollar level. He was bright, hardworking, and had excellent interpersonal skills. Matt was a relatively new advisor who sat in an office close to Ross, and the two began to share ideas and collaborate on an informal basis. Ross determined that Matt was "wicked smart" and liked that he had CFA designation. Although Matt had a much smaller practice, Ross recognized his need to raise his game in portfolio management and believed that Matt would be accretive to his practice because of his investment management skills and experience. They formalized their team and while Matt was at first given a smaller equity position, Ross was generous in increasing Matt's split over the years. Today they are very close to a fifty-fifty split and are running a $5 million practice.

Ross has continued to be the primary relationship manager for their top fifty relationships and oversees the business-development activities of the team. Matt is responsible for developing and overseeing the team's investment strategy and managing the core investment models. The team believes one of their strongest values to their clients is having Matt act as the portfolio manager. He has consistently outperformed the indexes, providing their clients with excellent long-term returns. The clients have direct access to Matt, which the team believes gives them a significant competitive advantage.

The potential partner roles on a horizontal team include:

- Investment strategist
- Business development
- Holistic planning
- Portfolio managers
- Asset management
- Intergenerational planning specialist
- Individuals
- Retirement plans
- Corporate executive specialist
- Retirement income specialist

Other non-partner roles for a horizontal team could include:

- **Investment associate.** Focused on planning, client relationships, or team management
- **Relationship manager.** Focused on smaller client relationships
- **Administrative manager.** Focused on top fifty clients

- **Client associate.** Focused on servicing smaller relationships
- **Operations associate.** Focused on administrative and operational needs of the team

PROS AND CONS OF A HORIZONTAL STRUCTURE

Positives

➤ Idea and decisionmaking sharing

➤ Succession planning

➤ Specialization that enables more expansive offerings

➤ Adds to capacity of team

➤ Better coverage when a partner is out

Negatives

➤ Equity splits require each partner to contribute more than their fair share

➤ Potential conflicts on equity splits

➤ Potential misunderstandings or personality conflicts

➤ More time required for team communication and decisionmaking

➤ Less autonomy for individual partners

Alliance Teams

The alliance team is characterized by two or more financial advisors who continue to run their own practices and collaborate for marketing and/or product specialization purposes. They also share administrative resources such as assistants, analysts, planners, etc. They do not pool assets and maintain separate FA production numbers. Accounts may be shared on a case-by-case basis.

In addition to having the advantages and disadvantages of a vertical or horizontal team depending on their structure, they must work to avoid issues concerning the use of the shared resources.

The shared resources are definitely a cost savings, provided the shared resources can handle the workloads of each advisor. This requires strong communication and a clearly defined agreement on how the FAs will share common resources.

An example of an alliance team was Ross and Pete. The strength of their practice was the successful discretionary asset management processes that they provided their clients. Pete's team already had a great deal of success in acquiring new affluent clients but Pete thought their investment process could be improved. Working with Ross, the new team developed an alliance structure that took advantage of their individual strengths. Pete hired Ross's team to provide asset management for his clients. They also went on joint prospecting appointments when Pete sourced high net worth prospects that he felt would benefit from Ross's asset management approach. When these new clients were acquired they split the business, with Pete acting as the relationship manager and Ross the asset manager.

PROS AND CONS OF AN ALLIANCE STRUCTURE

Positives

➤ An informal partner commitment to test the waters with the opportunity to formalize a more permanent team structure

➤ Ability to leverage different levels of expertise on a situational basis

Negatives

➤ Neither team is fully committed to the other's success

➤ No succession planning

Holistic Team

A holistic team merges vertical and horizontal team approaches, focusing on either a vertical or horizontal structure depending on the level of experience and revenue generated by the specialists involved. Finding the right people who will thrive in this environment can be challenging, especially if you are looking for a particular internal or external team member that has the depth of expertise needed. However, this is the team structure that is becoming more popular. The client experiences a total solution to satisfy all of her financial services needs, and this structure allows each team member to concentrate on his strengths and talents. For example, a senior financial advisor might want to add a junior partner that has expertise in planning, or in estate planning.

A great example of a holistic partnership is Mike and Bruce. Mike had established a successful wealth management practice that focused on providing planning with a goal-based approach. However, as his clientele's affluence increased, more sophisticated intergenerational and risk management solutions were needed. As a result, Mike hired Bruce, who had extensive insurance and risk-management experience.

Examples of internal partners that may be found on holistic teams are:

- Financial planners
- Investment specialists
- Insurance specialists
- Trust specialists

Examples of external partners used by holistic teams include:

- Attorneys
- CPAs/accountants

- Private bankers
- Commercial bankers
- Mortgage specialists

Other non-partner roles for a holistic team could include:

- **Investment associate.** Focused on planning, client relationships, or team management
- **Relationship manager.** Focused on smaller client relationships
- **Administrative manager.** Focused on top fifty clients
- **Client associate.** Focused on servicing smaller relationships
- **Operations associate.** Focused on administrative and operational needs of the team

PROS AND CONS OF A HOLISTIC STRUCTURE

Positives
- ➤ Clients are offered a holistic experience with total solutions.
- ➤ The model allows for specialization; everyone can do what they enjoy and do best.
- ➤ Clients view the team as a comprehensive provider.
- ➤ Offering holistic solutions creates extremely loyal clients.

Negatives
- ➤ They can be difficult to manage.
- ➤ Finding the right people to fill each role can be a challenge.
- ➤ This model has increased need for coordination of efforts, communication, and leadership.

TRY SITUATIONAL TEAMING

Situational teaming allows potential team members to work together before they make a decision to become an official team. In situational teaming, each FA gets to know each other, assess each other's professional values, and determine if they like and trust each other without making a full partnership commitment. Think of it as being like dating or living together before you make a marriage commitment.

Situational teaming typically begins when financial advisors work together to bring in a new client relationship, but it also can occur if FAs share clients for a variety of different reasons. This may occur when one financial advisor has a prospect but brings in another financial advisor who either has more experience or has an area of expertise that is needed to convert the prospect to a client. The individual financial advisors have the opportunity to work together, see each other in action, and evaluate the longer-term opportunities to form a team.

A situational team can be an ideal way for a senior advisor to consider adding a junior partner to the team without making a full commitment. In this case the senior advisor would agree to do joint prospect meetings together—helping the junior partner to close the deal while splitting the business. This is a win-win situation as the new advisor benefits from the experience and expertise of the senior advisor, and the senior advisor is provided the opportunity to get in front of new prospects sourced by the junior advisor.

Another example of situational teaming is when a senior partner gives another FA who is not part of her team some of her smaller relationships that no longer fit her team's minimum account size and splits that business with the junior FA. This is another win-win situation in that it allows the senior advisor to divest smaller relationships with another FA that she trusts, and the receiving FA gets business he doesn't have to source on his own.

FAMILY TEAMS

Bringing family members into a team is becoming a common practice. It makes sense the same way it would in any business: to have trusted family members be part of the business and eventually take it over. There are challenges that include perceived favoritism, undefined roles and responsibilities, and crossing the lines between the personal and professional relationships. Other team members might resent that a family member has a fast track and receives an unearned equity split. The best solution to this challenge is for the senior relative to make clear to the incoming family member that they must earn their way into an equity partner role through hard work, bringing in new business, and demonstrating their ability to work effectively with the team's existing clients and other team members. In short, family members need to be good team players and earn their place on the team.

However, the benefits of a family team can go far beyond succession planning and may include:

- Enjoyment of working with loved ones
- Bringing in a new and different perspective from someone you trust
- Technology skills the younger generation brings
- Opportunity to add professional designations such as CFP, CIMA, or CFA
- Ability to relate and effectively communicate with next generation of clients
- Opportunity to add depth of expertise to the team

It's important that the senior relatives be open minded to what the incoming family member can add to the team. Often, it's hard for parents to see their children as professionals. However, that professional respect is essential for the rest of the team members to see—and to give incoming family members the confidence they need to become valuable team members. Incoming family members need to be given very clear roles and responsibilities from the beginning. Examples could include being responsible for business development, being a relationship manager for the team's smaller clients, or being responsible for the financial planning division of the practice. Assigning specific roles and responsibilities to incoming family members provides them with the clarity and accountability required to demonstrate their abilities and contributions to the team.

Setting boundaries between the personal and professional relationship is also a best practice. Often family teams limit personal conversations to after office hours and do not refer to their parents or relatives as mom, dad, uncle, etc. at work.

JOINING OR MERGING EXISTING TEAMS

A common situation I see with my clients is when a team extends an invitation to merge with a sole practitioner or with another existing team. There are many good reasons for a merger to occur, but a common question I get from potential team clients is how to make the financials work for all parties.

The most common compensation scheme is for each team member (or sole practitioner) to determine their current equity split based on their share of the combined team. For example, if Joe is approached by a larger team to join them, and Joe is doing $1 million in business and the team approaching Joe is doing $2 million, than the combined production would be $3 million, and Joe's split would be 33 percent of the total. This legacy split would represent the foundation from which the combined team partners would get paid.

However, once the new team is formed the split could change. If Joe is younger than the other team members and they are bringing him in as part of a succession plan, he will later have more responsibility for the growth of the team than he might have now. Eventually he may be responsible for 50 percent of the growth of the combined practice. In this example, if the team grew from $3 million to $4 million, Joe's split would be 33 percent on the first $3 million and 50 percent of the next million (or $1.5 million total). His split would be closer to 40 percent once the growth component is factored in. This split incentivizes Joe to join the team and to engage in activities that will grow the total team's business. The partners of the other team benefit because, although their split will be proportionally less, their total income will be growing more than if they were on their own (because of the growth component that Joe is adding) and they will have a succession plan in place.

This is just one example of equity splits for merging teams and is designed to reflect the importance of incorporating a growth strategy into a senior team that may be plateaued and in need of a succession plan.

SUCCESSION PLANNING

When a new team is being formed a formal succession plan needs to be established. A succession plan assumes the team will succeed and outlines an orderly strategy so that the team can continue to function in perpetuity. This is different than a partnership agreement and dissolution process (which we'll discuss in the next section).

Chapter 3 covers the logistics and recommends a detailed process for a thoughtful succession plan. However, the details of the implementation of the succession plan does not have to be determined at the formation stage of the team; it just needs to be established what the succession plan will be and who will be part of it. In some cases, a team is formed just to have an orderly succession plan in place: That is a good reason for adding new FA partners to a team or for merging existing teams. It is very important for junior partners to know what role they will have in the succession plan. This provides both the motivation to join, and an incentive to make a long-term commitment to the team.

PARTNERSHIP AGREEMENTS AND
THE DISSOLUTION PROCESS

Going into a new team, every FA should be optimistic and committed to ensuring the newly formed team will be successful. Again, getting married is a good comparison—what newlywed couple doesn't believe that their marriage will last a lifetime? However, like some marriages, things happen. Often a team can work through their disagreements, conflicts, and challenges, but sometimes they can't be worked out. The closer aligned the individual FA partners' values are, the more likely that there will not be any dealbreaker issues. Ascertaining this is the point of the upfront discovery process.

The mindset of FAs joining a new team should be to expect the best but be prepared for the worst. In all cases the partnership agreement which includes the team dissolution agreement must be established prior to the formation of a new team, signed by all the partners, and then reviewed annually. The partnership agreement includes a strategy if issues can't be resolved or expectations are not met and the team decides to disband. Some examples could include the assignment of clients, what team members would go with each partner, and would there be any joint coverage of clients. Most firms have a standard partnership agreement that makes this process much easier.

BUILDING A HIGHLY FUNCTIONING TEAM
FROM SCRATCH

Moving from being a sole practitioner to the formation of a new team requires a significant commitment with far-reaching consequences and it needs to be taken very seriously. By incorporating best team practices in your newly formed team you are significantly increasing the probability of the team being highly functioning.

The following is a very short overview of team best practices as applied to the formation of a new team. Each of these best practices will be covered in depth in the following chapters. The needs of a newly formed team are different from an established team; the intent here is to guide you with a few key insights for the formation stage of team development.

- **Vision.** A newly formed team needs to develop a "team vision" that describes where the team wants to be in the long term, their ideal client profile, the reputation they want to have, and the ideal practice they want to be part of. Once the big picture vision is established, a three- to five-year year business plan needs to be developed to support the team's vision. This business plan acts as a blueprint or architectural design for building your dream house. Both the vision and business plan can be developed prior to formalizing a new team. This gives potential team members a chance to see in advance how aligned their potential team members' values are. It also gives everyone an opportunity to see each other in action and see how each person contributes to the vision and business plan.

- **Roles and responsibilities.** Newly formed teams need to determine the roles and responsibilities of their future team members in order to avoid potential duplication of roles. I recommend creating an organization chart of current partners, junior partners, specialists (investment and planning), relationship managers, administrative managers, and associates. This organization chart could also include proposed future team members. This exercise should be done prior to the formalization of the team.

- **Hiring and performance reviews.** Roles and responsibilities are meaningless without a consistent performance review process that ties directly to compensation. I strongly believe that accountability for roles and responsibilities needs to be assigned. Setting up a good performance measurement and review process takes time but it is essential to having a highly functioning team. Developing this process should be done as a high priority once the team has formed. The partners need to commit to semi-annual performance reviews for each team member, including themselves.

- **Compensation.** Compensating team members based on their performance is essential to driving the right behavior, retaining the team's best performers, and motivating team members to do more than their fair share. It is important in the team-formation process that the FA partners agree to a budget for compensation. This is part of ensuring that the partners' values are aligned, and that they are willing to invest back into their practice to ensure they have loyal, high-performing, and committed employees. This budget should be created prior to the final formation of the team. It is also important that the partners commit to having an annual partners' review, where each partner can make a case for equity split adjustments if warranted. The highest-functioning teams always have an open mind about rewarding the partners that make the biggest contributions—otherwise, the highest performers will not be incentivized to stay with the team. It is also essential to retaining junior partners that they earn a higher equity split through the contributions they make to the team's bottom line.

- **Communication.** A newly formed team should commit to formal team communication. A commitment to team communication is a core professional value that needs to be shared by all the FA partners of the team before the team formation is finalized.

- **Processes.** The highest-functioning teams in our industry are all highly process based. In the formation stage of teaming the partners should outline the necessary processes. The next step is to evaluate the processes that each FA team partner is bringing to the newly formed team. Then, team processes need to be reviewed periodically to evaluate their effectiveness. I recommend that potential teams evaluate their existing processes prior to the formal team formation so these processes are ready to implement from day one.

■ **Leadership.** Strong team leadership is essential in order to create a highly functioning team. As the team is being formed it should be determined who the team leader will be, along with that leader's responsibilities and compensation. (The most common compensation for a team leader is an increased team pool equity split to compensate for the time and energy required to be an effective team leader. This is not necessarily a large split increase but enough to make the team leadership role worthwhile.) In a vertical team structure the team leader would typically default to the senior partner. However, being a strong team leader is not necessarily a skill that all partners have. It is important to note that seniority is not necessarily the most important consideration for selecting the team leader. I have seen many instances when a junior team member is more qualified to be a team leader than the most senior partner.

ANNOUNCE YOUR TEAM TO ALL

It is a best practice to announce the formation of the new team to the team's clients. A formal announcement should be made and communicated through email, and the team's best clients should be called individually by each of the FAs responsible for those clients to share the news, outline the benefits, and introduce new team members.

Another best practice is to host an open house in which the best clients are invited to personally meet the new team.

THE NEXT STEP

In the next chapter, you'll learn the first of my team best practices: creating and maintaining a vision, and how developing a thoughtful business plan is one of the best ways to codify that vision.

3

Create a Vision

According to Maxwell Maltz, the renowned author who wrote *Psycho Cybernetics,* the greatest fulfillment people get in life is from the achievement of goals that are important to them. There is no question people are motivated by big goals and a clear vision on how to achieve those goals. In all industries, the most productive people are relentlessly persistent, strongly oriented toward goals, and take responsibility for their results.

One of the team best practices is providing team members with a clear vision to achieve the team's goals. In a recent study by Moss Adams, one of the fifteen largest public accounting and consulting firms, when leadership is accompanied by clear goals and a sense of purpose, team productivity is boosted by 24 percent.

In order to have a productive and engaged work environment it is essential to have a clearly defined vision for the team. Setting a vision and accomplishing important goals provides meaning; it bolsters the day-to-day (often mundane) work and makes it seem as if you are working toward something bigger. It also drives the daily activities and tactics of individual team members. The team members need to know how their daily activities, assignments, and tasks connect to a plan.

Surprisingly, a 2014 survey conducted for FA Insights by Design Study showed that only 17 percent of advisors had developed a strategic plan regardless if they were on a team or not. The irony of this survey is that most advisors would not invest their clients' assets without having developed financial plans for those clients, yet most don't have a business plan for themselves. The fact is that most advisors are better at planning their clients' futures than their own.

The most productive teams in our industry embrace the importance of providing their team members with big goals and a vision to achieve them. This vision is communicated to every team member and reiterated regularly. The team vision lets team members know where the team leaders want to take the team and puts them in position to reach that destination. Without this vision, individual team members are just doing a series of tasks without any meaning or purpose.

Equally as important as setting big goals and having a vision to achieve these goals is consistent accountability regarding progress made toward the achievement of those goals. Without accountability, establishing goals and a vision becomes an academic exercise that has little impact on the morale and productivity of the team members. In other words, it totally defeats the purpose.

DEVELOPMENT OF A VISION

The first step in establishing the team vision is to establish the big goals the team wants to reach in the medium term. The timeframe that I use when coaching advisors is typically five years. These big goals always include business generated (revenue), total dollars under investment (assets), a target number of affluent clients, and a number of prospects in the pipeline. However, all the teams I interviewed have goals that go beyond these basics in developing a team vision. Many of the best practicing teams included quality of life goals in their visions. Examples might include more vacation time, sabbaticals, or time off during the week. These teams recognize that a good balance between personal and professional lives is essential, and goals need to be established for both.

Some of the goals best practicing teams include in their team visions:

1. New affluent clients brought in
2. Assets
3. Total number of affluent clients
4. Ideal client profile and minimums
5. Loyal client service model
6. Ideal prospect profile
7. Number of affluent prospects
8. Future value proposition
9. Ideal wealth management offering
10. Infrastructure of the practice
11. Number of client relationships and average size
12. Specialization
13. Reputation
14. Responsible citizenship contributions
15. Number of team members and their future roles

CREATE A VISION AND BUSINESS PLAN BEFORE FORMALIZING YOUR TEAM

For many advisors considering building or joining a team, the vision and business plan can be developed prior to formalizing the new team. This gives potential team members a chance to see in advance how aligned their potential team members' values are. It also gives potential team members the opportunity to see each other in action and how each person contributes to the vision and business plan.

" We also look at different goals—how often were we able to ski, fish, or golf with clients? How many Fridays were we able to take off and not spend at work? How many days did we work until 6:00 during the middle of the week? So, we are not just looking at business metrics but also stress level, and time with clients."

—Charles and Steve

TO CREATE A VISION, START WITH A BUSINESS PLAN

The business plan transforms a vision into a reality. It establishes a blueprint for how the team vision will be achieved. The vision is what your dream house will look like, and the business plan is the blueprint to build the house.

My first insight into the power of a business plan came when I first started as a professional coach. I had retired from Merrill Lynch in 2007 and started a business training financial advisors. One of the financial advisors, who I had hired twenty-five years earlier and who subsequently built a highly successful practice contacted me and asked me to coach him on how to lead his team. When I started the training company I had envisioned training groups of financial advisors, not individual advisors. So when my friend asked me to coach his team I agreed, assuming it would be pro bono work. However, he insisted on paying me to be his coach. Now the pressure was on: I had to develop a formal FA coaching offering, which I didn't have.

I decided that the best coaching model would be the same way the best FAs work with their clients. The first step would be a deep discovery of where their team was now and what their goals and priorities for the future were. Based on that discovery I would develop a business plan to guide the FA toward reaching the team's goals. Once the business plan was developed, I would coach the FA on a monthly basis to help him implement the business plan to reach the team's goals, focusing on the highest priority goals first. The business plan to the FA was the same as a financial plan to a client.

I have since used the same coaching process with hundreds of individual financial advisors through my firm, Altius Learning. I have determined that one of the most productive things an FA team can do is to develop a business plan and implement it. The reason the development and implementation of a business plan is such a powerful tool is that implementing a business plan transforms a team from being reactive to proactive. Consistently doing the right activities leads to the right results.

The research on teams validates my experience. According to research done by CEG, 73 percent of the highest-performing advisory teams have a business plan in place. Yet according to a recent Financial Planning Association (FPA) survey, less than 33 percent of all advisor teams have a written plan. Additionally, the survey found that only 13 percent of advisors felt they had control of their time—and those that did attributed that control to having a business plan.

The FPA survey also asked advisory teams to list the five most important things that contributed to the growth of their practice. When they tallied the results, the second most frequent answer was "create a plan with written goals and use it to develop a written strategy on where they need to be in two, five, and ten years."

CREATING THE BUSINESS PLAN

The business plan and its implementation become the centerpiece for team communication, team roles, and job descriptions. The business plan takes a seat at the table in team meetings and is used by the team leaders to clarify expectations for every member of the team. In summary, the business plan defines where the team is now, where the team wants to go, how to get there, and every team member's role in achieving the team vision.

A business plan doesn't have to be elaborate or formal—it can simply be an outline of action steps and prioritization of those action steps for each area of a team's practice. When I work with a team to develop their business plan, the first step is to diagnose the current state of their practice. Most financial advisors would agree that this is similar to the discovery phase when they are working with a new client—it establishes the baseline. Teams should diagnose the current state of their team, grading themselves in each area of their practice. Each area being diagnosed and analyzed is prioritized based on its importance in achieving goals determined by the team vision. After an honest assessment of the team's strengths and weaknesses, specific action steps can be developed to achieve the goals outlined in the team vision. These action steps can then be assigned to different team members—with measurements developed to ensure the actions are being completed. Finally, communicate the process with the entire team. Everyone should be aware of progress on the action steps and results as they relate to the team's goals in each area. This simple process of diagnosis, development of action steps, prioritization, assignment to team members, measurement, and communication of progress is the basis for the business plan.

> **" We don't look at month over month—we look at rolling quarters and our objective is to have consistent growth."**
>
> —*Charles and Steve*

BUSINESS PLANNING BEST PRACTICE ANALYSIS

This book is designed to provide you with tangible action steps needed for all the team-related areas in the business plan. There is a chapter for each of these team best practices that provides complete guidance on how to implement them. By identifying the areas of your team that need improvement, you can skip directly to that chapter and be provided with all the action steps needed to address that challenge.

That's the purpose of this chapter and the remainder of the book—to give you everything you need to transform your team into a highly functioning best practice team.

Let's start by using the following diagnosis process to evaluate your existing team. By looking at each of the best practices from this vantage point, you will clearly see the areas of your team that need improvement.

- **Vision.** There are four goals that every team should include in their vision and their business plan: business growth, asset growth, affluent client household growth, and prospect pipeline. The success in achieving these goals will determine the growth rate of the team. While other goals are important, these are essential. The team should then determine the following: have we set goals (including the four essential goals), are we measuring them, have we assigned responsibility, and are we communicating the results.

- **Roles and responsibilities.** The essential divisions within a team should be clearly outlined in the business plan. These divisions should include the team's offering, services, and marketing. Best practicing teams have assigned specific roles and responsibilities to each team member to cover those essential divisions. These roles and responsibilities should be codified to include essential activities and goals. A controller needs to be established for each team to measure the results assigned to each team member, which will be the basis for the performance evaluation and compensation. Finally, it is essential that the team is organized to enable the partners or team leaders to focus primarily on the essential activities: development and implementation of the team's wealth management process (the offering), contact with affluent clients (services), and business development (marketing). All other activities should be delegated to other team members.

- **Performance.** An essential part of the vision process and the creation of the business plan is defining the difference between excellent, acceptable, and unacceptable levels of performance. In assigning goals to team members, the focus should be setting three to five goals that compensation is based on. Limit the number to no more than five. Best practicing teams do semiannual reviews with each team member and have established templates for mid-year and end-of-year reviews.

- **Communication.** Best team practices include having a short daily meeting (ten to fifteen minutes) to review the tactical issues of each day, a weekly team meeting (one hour) that focuses on less urgent but important tactical issues the team faces, and semiannual offsite meetings focused on the strategic areas for the team to improve (half day). Best practicing teams have established agenda templates for their weekly and semiannual meetings. They also assign a member of the team to lead the weekly meetings. (Often this rotates between team members.) These meetings need to be outlined in the business plan.

  Another team communication best practice is to get input in advance of the team meetings and incorporate that input in the meeting's agenda. I also recommend assigning note-taking responsibility to a team member and having that person summarize team meetings and share the summary with all team members after the meeting. Summaries should include action items, timelines for completion, and assignment of responsibilities to a team member.

- **Compensation.** Compensation strategies need to be outlined in a business plan. Best practicing teams base compensation on controllable results and activities. They also are very generous to loyal high performers, consistently paying them in the top 25 percent of comparable earners. As a guideline, the top advisor compensates her team between 7.5 and 15 percent of her income. Nonproducing team members are paid a combination of base salary, an individual performance bonus, and a team performance bonus.

  Best practicing teams also look for ways to provide recognition beyond compensation for outstanding work by individual team members. Recognition is a powerful motivator. Finally, a team best practice is to have an annual partner's compensation meeting to review partners' splits, expense pools, and to update the team succession plan.

- **Hiring.** To be a top-performing team you must have a process for sourcing, hiring, and training new team members, and all of these activities need to be outlined in your business plan. Best practicing teams typically have a ninety-day probationary period to evaluate performance and attitude of new team members and can terminate team members who fail to meet expectations. Teams should go through an annual evaluation for personnel growth and determine if new team members need be brought in as financial advisors, administrative employees, or relationship managers. One of the recommended exercises that each partner should go through is to determine what activities they regularly engage in that are not essential (see *roles and responsibilities* on p. 47) and make sure there is a team member they can delegate those activities to.

- **Offering.** Best practicing teams have established a world-class wealth management offering that has a high appeal to affluent individuals. They have spent time and effort to establish a consistent, repeatable process. By consistently improving their offering they know they will separate themselves from their competition, attracting more highly affluent individuals in their market. Just as important as developing a world-class management offering is being able to articulate how their offering is different and the value they provide to their clients: the value proposition.

- **Marketing.** Does the team have consistent and proactive business-development strategies designed to bring in additional assets and new affluent clients? There are seven core acquisition strategies that the best acquiring teams employ: proactive client referrals, developing a professional referral network, event marketing, developing a niche, transition strategies to move affluent acquaintances to prospects, acquiring client assets held away, and developing and managing a prospect pipeline.

- **Process.** Best practicing teams have developed a process-based team practice. They recognize that having quality, consistent, and repeatable processes for every team function and activity greatly enhances productivity. A best practice is to organize processes by division of the practice. The divisions that each team should have include wealth management (product), service, marketing, and human resources (internal team practices). It is recommended that as a team you evaluate your existing processes for each of these departments and decide if they need to be improved. Determine which processes you need that you don't have currently. Then assign responsibility to improve and develop needed processes. A new process should be evaluated sixty days after it has been improved or added.

- **Leadership.** Having strong leadership within the team is essential to a highly functioning team. The team must establish a team leader. That team leader needs to incorporate the seven essential leadership principles: well-defined hiring and training practices, accountability, integrity, providing a vision, recognition, effective communication, and being a good decisionmaker.

" Our business plan is a playbook and it's the same playbook we ran this year, the year before, the year before, and the year before that. We tweak it all the time but in general it works perfectly."

—*Charles and Steve*

TEAM BUSINESS ANALYSIS

There are a number of other areas that teams should evaluate themselves on that are not related to team practices. This is not an all-inclusive list but represents some other areas in which to diagnose and evaluate your team.

- **Infrastructure.** Has the team determined how many clients, or households, each team member can effectively work with? If the team is working with too many, have they established effective divesture strategies? Also has the team segmented their households and assigned the smaller households to a relationship manager?

- **Business efficiency.** Does the team have an established process for capturing complete wallet share for their core affluent client base? Wallet share includes outside assets as well as providing for all of the client's financial services needs—including asset protection, intergenerational planning, and liability management.

- **Fiduciary pricing.** Has the team committed to fiduciary (fee-based) pricing and developed strategies to increase their fee-based pricing? These strategies need to include transitioning transactional-based clients to fiduciary pricing.

- **Professional development.** Does every member of the team have a plan to further develop their skills? Examples could include obtaining a CFP or a CIMA designation, developing niche expertise, building a practice management reading list, joining a peer sharing group to learn from colleagues, or (for nonpartners) becoming registered.

- **Budget.** A budget needs to be established for how much the team is going to invest back into the practice (retained earnings). Examples of expenditures could include marketing and travel expenses, hiring new team members, compensation for team members, and recognition for team members.

- **Service model.** World-class service is essential to a highly functioning team committed to growth. A service model needs to be established and maintained that provides extraordinary service to the team's best clients. The service model needs to include frequency of contact, Wow moments, a problem resolution process, onboarding, and in-depth client profiling.

- **Time management.** To be a highly functioning team the partners must establish and follow the proven time management practices of delegation, prioritization, and time blocking. The partners on the team must be committed to devoting at least 50 percent of their time to contacting their top fifty clients and to business development activities.

BUSINESS ANALYSIS CHECKLIST FOR DIAGNOSING YOUR CURRENT TEAM'S PRACTICES

Infrastructure

- ❑ Identify the number of households you can effectively work with.
- ❑ Do you need to segment your clients?
- ❑ If applicable, what are your divesture strategies?

Business Efficiency

- ❑ Do you believe you are running an efficient practice?
- ❑ Create a strategy for working toward 100 percent wallet share with your affluent clients.
- ❑ Establish minimums for your client in terms of assets and annual business.

Fiduciary Pricing

- ❑ What percentage of your practice is fee-based?
- ❑ Create fee-based goals for this year.
- ❑ Create a strategy of moving transactional-based clients to fiduciary pricing.

Business-Development Strategies

- ❑ Determine how to fit business development strategies into your daily schedule.

Professional Development

- ❑ What are your plans to further develop your expertise as a financial advisor?
- ❑ Do you have any plans to obtain a professional designation?

Budget

- ❑ Identify a dollar amount to commit to retained earnings to support the growth of your practice.
- ❑ Identify sources of income to help you meet your budget needs (for example, firm, local branch, strategic partner). How much do you expect to receive?

Service Model

❑ Do you provide an exceptional service experience to your best clients?

❑ Who is responsible for that delivery?

Time Management

❑ Are you committed to finding time in your daily schedule for activities that will grow your practice?

BUSINESS PLAN WORKSHEET

Once the diagnosis of the team has been completed, the next step is to determine what action steps need to be taken to improve certain areas. The action steps should be outlined under each area. The purpose of the business plan outline worksheet is to provide a tool that lets you write out action steps the team is committed to taking under each of the areas. The process of diagnosing your current team practice, developing action steps to improve each area, and transferring those action steps to the business plan outline work-sheet results in development of a business plan. You can make it more formal if you want, but formality is less important than developing an action step outline that is in effect a business plan.

Altius Learning Business Plan Worksheet

The following is an example of a business plan worksheet related to team practices that was filled in by one of my clients:

- **Vision.** Our team has a long-term vision of where we would like to be. We have not developed a business plan to reach that vision. This is a high priority that we would like to have completed by Q1.

- **Roles and responsibilities.** We have established general roles and responsibilities but have not organized them by the big three essential activities: our offering, service, and sales. Going forward we will do that. The partners need to give up more of the non-$500 tasks and delegate them to the rest of the team. We will also have written job descriptions for each team member. This is a medium priority that we would like to have done by mid-year.

- **Performance reviews.** Because we have not had detailed and written job descriptions we have not consistently done performance reviews but will start doing them by the second half of the year. This is a medium priority for us.

- **Communication.** We have done a good job with this and have had daily and weekly team meetings. We have not done strategic meetings and will begin to add this to our team communications. Improving communications is a lower priority for us since we currently have team communication covered well. Our goal would be to do a strategic meeting by the end of next year.

- **Compensation.** Our compensation for our non-FA team members is now entirely subjective. We are committed to adding formal job descriptions and measurable criteria. This will become the basis for a more objective and fair compensation structure. We will start this process next year. This is a medium priority for our team, tied to establishing roles and responsibilities and performance reviews.

- **Hiring.** We really like the idea of the relationship manager role and believe it would work for our team. We have too many small relationships and this position would solve how we handle these smaller relationships. We have a senior client associate that would fit the job description. This is a high priority and we would like to add this position to our team in the next month.

- **Offering.** We have spent a great deal of time refining our value proposition which we are very comfortable with.

- **Marketing.** We will implement a marketing program based on a proactive referral process, six prospect and client events a year, developing transition strategies to turn affluent personal acquaintances into prospects, and building relationships with our clients' CPAs to generate referrals. This is all in order to build out our prospect pipeline.

- **Processes.** We have not been running a process-based team outside of our investment process. We plan on using the gap analysis tool to determine what processes we need to add to our practice. This is a high priority that we are committed to starting immediately.

- **Leadership.** Our team has not exhibited strong leadership in the past. However, we feel that incorporating the needed team best practices into our business plan will greatly improve the leadership of our team.

PRIORITIZING YOUR ACTIONS

The final stage of the business plan process is prioritizing the areas that are most important to the team. Formalize the plan outline worksheet into a written business plan and then review the business plan with the team. After I develop a business plan for a financial advisor coaching client and review the plan with the client, I always get the same reaction from every team I work with: Members of the team, while complimenting me for developing the business plan, always state that they feel overwhelmed by all the things they feel they need to do that are recommended in the business plan.

Over the years, I have learned to break the business plan into parts and focus on making changes in one area at a time, with the objective of implementing the entire business plan within twelve months. This process ensures that the team will not be overwhelmed and will have realistic expectations for implementing the business plan within a year of developing it.

IMPLEMENTING YOUR BUSINESS PLAN

As powerful as establishing a vision and developing a business plan can be, if steps aren't taken to implement the plan, the power of the vision will be lost. As I like to say: A vision without action is a dream, action without vision is wasted, but vision and action together turn dreams into reality.

The biggest challenge in the business planning process is not the development of a business plan, but rather the successful implementation of it. The first step in successful implementation of the business plan is communicating it and selling it to all the team members. The business plan ties the individual team members into one team working toward something big and important; every team member will benefit from the business plan if it is successfully implemented. Not only should the vision be shared along with the business plan (as the blueprint to reach it) once it is developed—it should also be referenced during team meetings throughout the year. It should take a seat at the table at every team meeting and be the "team constitution" that guides daily team actions and priorities.

The next step in the successful implementation of the business plan is assigning responsibility to individual team members to ensure that the business plan gets done. An example could be improving the client service experience. One of the action steps might be to create a client profile to determine a client's outside interests, the most special day in her life, her passions, her children and grandchildren's names. That action step could be assigned to a client associate to organize the client profile and make sure it is completed by the associate and the FA who is responsible for that client. Once that in-depth client profile has been completed another action step would be to create

"Wow moments" throughout the year by taking the client profile information and acting on it in a way that builds closer relationships with the client. Examples of Wow moments could include acknowledging the "most important day of a client's life" with a small gift and a handwritten note or inviting her to an event that she has a strong interest in or developing deeper relationships with her children. The client associate responsible for completing the client profile and creating the Wow moments should also be given a timeframe for completing those tasks and reporting to the team controller when those tasks are completed. The client associate that is assigned those tasks is implementing the actions steps outlined in developing a world-class service model.

Once business plan tasks are assigned and deadlines established, make sure to recognize and reward team members for their work. Recognition can be given during team meetings and during the semi-annual performance reviews that become the basis for bonuses and raises. In the case of financial advisors being assigned tasks related to the business plan, recognition should be given and compensation will naturally increase as the business plan contributes to the growth of the team.

FOCUS ON SUCCESSION PLANNING

Team succession planning is a very important component of team best practices and is part of providing and implementing a team vision. I will make a strong statement by saying that *all teams need to have a succession plan—period.*

I can think of no valid reason that a team could give me for not having a succession plan in the event of a partner leaving the team. In many ways, it's like having life insurance—you may not need it right away, but it's always good to have when you do.

Once a succession plan is made it can be changed or fine-tuned as needed. While a succession plan is a necessity, it doesn't need to be written in stone; it can and should be changed as circumstances dictate. The objective is for the team to go on in perpetuity and be bigger than any individual team member. For that to happen a succession plan is required.

It's interesting that according to a 2014 SEI advisory survey, only 20 percent of the advisors surveyed had an executable continuity plan. If my strong recommendation is that *all* teams have a succession plan and only 20 percent of teams have one, then there is a lot of room for improvement in succession planning for most teams. More than half of all financial advisors are over fifty. Impending retirement is a reality for these advisors, but only a minority have prepared their team for that eventuality.

Succession Planning Guidelines

- **Introduction.** As a standard practice, all the individual clients of a team should know each team member and what their roles and responsibilities are. This should be done whenever a new client is onboarded as well as when new team members are added.

- **Reviews.** Doing occasional joint reviews with other team members gives each of the partner's clients an opportunity to get to know each of the other partners professionally and start to build the level of trust needed for a succession plan to be effective. As a senior team member gets closer to retirement the team member that will be responsible for the client after the senior member retires needs to be part of the reviews on a more frequent basis and take a lead role during the reviews.

- **Call backs.** When a top fifty client calls the senior partner, she should periodically defer the call back to a junior partner so that the client can get used to the junior partner being responsive to his needs. Passing down the call provides the opportunity for the junior partner to get to know the client better.

- **Client assignment.** The senior partner should assign some of her clients to the junior partner to be the primary relationship manager for those clients.

- **Events.** Building trust between the team's best clients and other team members means getting to know the team members personally as well as professionally. The personal relationships between the team advisors and clients can be enhanced by having multiple team advisors participate in the smaller, intimate events that each of the partners has for their clients.

- **Retirement.** In the year before the senior partner's retirement there should be a formal announcement of the planned retirement to the clients who will be impacted telling them who they will be assigned to (another financial advisor or relationship manager). This allows the retiring partner to ensure a successful transition to the assigned advisor. If the other guidelines are followed the client should have already built a relationship with the assigned advisor before the retirement of the senior advisor is formally announced, ensuring a relatively seamless transition.

Succession planning should not be a taboo subject; in fact it should be transparent at all times. The very nature of being on a team is that there is a built-in succession plan but making sure that succession plan is formalized and transparent to all the significant clients of the team is vital. From a client's standpoint, it is reassuring that they know they will be taken care of by the team as their financial advisor goes through life transitions (death, retirement, illness).

TEAM BEST PRACTICES VISION CHECKLIST

- ❏ Is there a clearly defined five-year vision for the team?
- ❏ Has each partner agreed and committed to the team vision and goals?

❑ Has the team set annual goals that will result in achievement of the five-year vision?

❑ Are the goals tracked on a monthly or quarterly basis? Who is responsible for tracking them? Has a controller position been established?

❑ How will the results be communicated to other team members?

❑ Has compensation and recognition been aligned with goals being reached?

❑ Has the team developed a business plan to reach the five-year vision?

❑ Has the team determined the gaps between the five-year vision and where the team is today?

❑ Has the team developed action steps to address these gaps?

❑ Have the action steps been prioritized and assigned to a specific team member?

❑ How will the results of the action steps being completed be communicated to the team members?

4

Assigning Roles and Responsibilities

Best practicing teams are very deliberate about the roles and responsibilities they assign to members of their team. They frequently evaluate what roles are required to assure that the team is performing at a high level. In the research that Altius has done with the thousands of advisors we have trained and coached, we have found the best-performing teams have clearly defined roles and responsibilities.

FOUR ESSENTIAL DIVISIONS OF LABOR

The question that many advisors have when determining the roles and responsibilities of their team is where to start, and how to ensure that all the teams' needs are covered. I have found that the best-performing and highest-functioning teams operate the same way a successful business would in any industry. As I help teams to get this right, I recommend that they think of their practice as a business. If you look at any successful business, they typically have four essential divisions: products, service, human resources, and marketing. As a team develops the roles and responsibilities needed, they should organize around the needs of each of the four divisions.

The Product Division

This is the business's offering, it's what the client pays them for—it's their goods and services. In financial services the product is your wealth management offering and your expertise. The wealth management offering includes your discovery process to determine your clients' risk tolerance and goals. It includes the development of a financial plan that provides the blueprint for reaching those goals. It also includes your investment process—model portfolios, asset managers, buy-sell disciplines, and the many other aspects of portfolio management. It can include intergenerational planning, risk management, and liability management. Finally, it includes timely financial reviews and statements to evaluate progress toward goals—and making necessary adjustments as needed. The degree to which this wealth management process is done will vary from team to team, but like any business, the more successful the product, the more in demand it will be. The best providers will be paid a premium for their offering.

The Service Division

All successful businesses are committed to providing their clients with outstanding customer service. The objective should be to have loyal and "raving fan" clients and developing and implementing a world-class service model is essential to reaching that objective. For instance, I own a Lexus and I'm planning to buy a new car in the near future. I have looked at and read many reviews on a number of different brands and types of cars. But as I contemplate what car to buy I keep coming back to thinking about buying another Lexus. The reason is not just that it's a nice car, but that the service department of our local Lexus dealership is extraordinary. Not only do they provide great maintenance, they always have a loaner car, the service reps go out of their way to be helpful, they always fit me in when I have an emergency, and they have a wonderful waiting area that includes work spaces, refreshments, and great ambiance. No matter what other car I can consider I don't think any other dealership would provide the same level of great service. After a few weeks of searching I decided that my next car will be another Lexus.

In financial services, the same is true: Many advisor firms provide solid investment advice and wealth management, but the difference between a satisfied client and a "raving fan" is the service experience.

The Human Resources Division

This is where every business focuses on their employees. Small businesses often don't have a designated HR person, but whoever is handling these tasks is focused on the hiring and training procedures of the firm. HR determines the roles and responsibilities of the employees, the performance measurements and review process of the employees, and the team's recognition and compensation practices, including benefits. It is also the division of the business that oversees the employees, ensuring that the team gets the best from them.

The Marketing Division

This division focuses on promoting the product and attracting new clients. Every FA business should have an ideal client profile and build their marketing division around the acquisition of those types of clients to the business. In financial services, the marketing division should have some combination of the following seven business development strategies: client referrals, building a professional referral network, event marketing, transitioning personal relationships to clients, bringing in existing clients' assets held away, niche marketing, and building and managing a prospect pipeline. Additionally, the marketing division develops the value proposition and branding of the practice through websites, marketing collateral, and social media.

Most advisor teams have decent product and service divisions. Some teams have adequate human resources divisions but most don't. However very, very few advisory teams have *any* type of marketing division. The reality is that the vast majority of experienced advisors simply rely on reactive marketing strategies like unsolicited referrals and unsolicited consolidation of assets from existing clients.

A financial advisory team will never reach their full potential without a proactive and robust marketing division committed to attracting new, ideal clients. The same would be true with any business in any industry: The most successful businesses proactively market to their ideal clientele.

DIVISIONAL ROLES AND RESPONSIBILITIES

The following lists suggest which type of employee can handle the work for each division. Each division does not need all of these employees: These are simply suggestions as to who would be qualified for the tasks at hand, and appropriate job titles. In some cases, the same role was assigned to different divisions. This reflects that an individual team member might have responsibilities in different divisions *or* that when there are multiple team members with the same role or level, they might be each assigned primary responsibility for a different division.

Finally, standards and expectations need to be set for each of these roles. Tasks should be set and evaluations made of those team members assigned to those roles and responsibilities based on an assumption of high performance.

Product Division
- Partner
- Relationship Manager
- Specialist
- Next Generation Planner
- Investment Analyst
- Financial Planner

Service Division
- Partner
- Relationship Manager

- Registered Client Associate
- Administrative Assistant
- Investment Associate
- Concierge Manager

Marketing Division
- Partner
- Business Development Associate
- Marketing Manager

Human Resources Division
- Partner
- Business Manager COO
- Controller

THREE ESSENTIAL JOBS

Most FAs spend too much time on tasks that can be delegated. As a result, not enough time is spent on the most productive activities. I believe there are a number of reasons (or deeply held beliefs) that cause this dynamic:

- Nobody can do this job as well as I can.
- I can't afford to have a mistake made with my big clients.
- It takes too much time to teach someone else how to do it.
- I'd rather do a less important task than prospect.
- I don't have anyone on my team to give this task to.

A better way to look at this issue is to assign a billable rate to the tasks a financial advisor can't delegate. The approximate billable hourly rate for an advisor that is tied to their production is as follows:

$1,000,000 in production = $500/hour
$2,000,000 in production = $1,000/hour
$3,000,000 in production = $1,500/hour

I believe there are only three tasks that a financial advisor cannot delegate. I call these "the big three," and they include:

1. The development and implementation of their wealth management process—the client experience (product division)
2. The contact—face and voice time with their top fifty client relationships (service division)
3. Business development activities that result in the acquisition of new affluent clients and assets (marketing division)

Engaging in these tasks is the "billable hourly rate" of the FA production level, whether that is $500, $1,000, or $1,500.

Tasks that can be delegated to an administrative member of the team should cost approximately $30/hour. If I can get an FA to look at their billable hourly rate and compare it to the hourly rate of an administrative team member the light bulb switches on, and they see how important the delegation of nonessential tasks can be.

Beyond the big three, every other task is tied to a billable hourly rate of $30/hour.

A financial advisor only has so much time and energy to give every day, and the more time and energy is spent on the big three, the more the FA will be compensated. It should be clear to any financial advisor that goes through this analysis that the more $30 work they do, the less $500 work they have time for and less profitable they are every day.

Imagine that your team has more tasks to do than any one person has time for, and a very experienced administrative manager is available because the advisor she works for is retiring. You interview her and discover she has more than enough experience and skills to do everything you need. When you ask her what kind of salary she is looking for, she tells you that she wants $500 per hour. Can you afford to hire her? The truth is you already have someone at that level—it's *you.* If you are spending time doing non-big three tasks you are your own assistant. Pass up the $500 assistant and hire one for $30/hour.

If you want to take your team's practice to the next level, the majority of your time needs to be spent on the things you are uniquely qualified to do. If something can be outsourced, delegated, or eliminated, do so. This is one of the most critical factors that sets top advisors apart. The top advisors spend 50 to 75 percent of their time doing just two things: proactive business development and client contact. Most advisors spend less than 20 percent on these revenue-producing activities.

HOW ARE YOU SPENDING YOUR TIME?

When a team determines specific roles and responsibilities that are needed for the team, the roles needed to be divided in two ways:

1. Big three activities = $500/hour+
2. Non-big three activities = $30/hour

Have each FA write down all the non-big three tasks they do each day for a week. Combine these lists: This becomes the job description for an administrative member of the team.

If you already have an admin, see how many of these tasks that person is doing, or has the capacity to do. If the administrative staff has the capacity to do more of these tasks, assign it to them. If not, hire an additional team member to do them. More often than not, the administrative team members have the capacity to do more, but because advisors on the team don't delegate enough they are underutilized.

Often a deterrent against hiring a new team member is cost. However, the reality is the financial advisors pay a new team member $30/hour so they can do more $500/hour work—it's a $470 an hour arbitrage and that math works every time. I have never worked with a financial advisory team that added a needed administrative person that regretted the additional cost. It has one of the highest ROIs of any investment a team can make.

JOB DESCRIPTIONS AND GOALS

One of the best team practices as it relates to roles and responsibilities is to have written job descriptions for each team member. One of the exercises that I do when coaching teams is to ask team members to write down what they believe is their primary job function. Once each member of the team has written what they believe are their job descriptions I meet with the entire team and share the descriptions that each member wrote. Then I ask the team, *"Has every job that is important to the team functioning at a high level been covered?"*

In most cases, the team will collectively respond that some task is missing. Those missing tasks need to be assigned to an existing team member. Or, if there are enough missing tasks, a new team member needs to be hired. Next, we rank the tasks in priority order, and either assign it to a member of the team that has capacity or develop a job description for an additional team member.

Performance and compensation are based on how well the team member performs on the high-priority tasks assigned. As a guideline, assign three to five measurable high-priority tasks to each team member. (This process will be covered in more detail in later chapters.)

The following are typical job descriptions for a financial services team:

TEAM JOB DESCRIPTIONS

FINANCIAL ADVISOR #1

1. **Team Leader**

   Team executive committee head

   Strategic vision

   Hiring

   Coordinate team responsibilities

   Conduct performance reviews

2. **Investments**

   Portfolio construction (with FA #2)

   Responsible for most sophisticated option, hedging, and
   Al strategies

3. **Business Development**

   Prospect meetings

   Main presenter

   Closer

4. **Client Relationships**

   Relationship manager for top fifty clients

FINANCIAL ADVISOR #2

1. **Client Relationships**

   Client reviews and communication with second-tier clients

2. **Investments**

   Portfolio management and investment strategy

   Research conference calls

   Performance monitoring

3. **Business Management—Controller**

   Tracking results versus goals

Outsource to other FAs

Team payouts

4. **Business Development (secondary)**

Building relationships with clients, CPAs, and attorneys as
potential referrals sources

FINANCIAL ADVISOR #3

1. **Business Development—Sourcing Leads and Prospects**

Cold calling highly qualified affluent prospects

COI meetings and events

Event marketing

New prospect meetings

Pipeline management

2. **Client Relationships (Secondary)**

Client contacts—smaller relationships

In-person meetings and reviews with assigned clients

CLIENT ASSOCIATE #1

Team expense monitoring

Client planning preparation

Client review preparation

Client review scheduling

Technology person for team

Back up for administrative tasks and for clients

CLIENT ASSOCIATE #2

Client administration for core affluent clients (top 100)

Fifty touch points for top fifty clients

TEAM BEST PRACTICES POTENTIAL ROLES

In my thirty-seven years of working with teams and observing and interviewing many of the highest-functioning teams in our industry, I have seen a variety of different roles and responsibilities. The following is a description of key roles and responsibilities in each of the four divisions. Not every team should have all of these roles, but this list will give you a broad spectrum of potential roles to consider. Each of these roles has proven to be a valuable part of a highly functioning team.

- **Partner.** Equity owner and financial advisor job description—typically senior advisor—product, service, HR, and marketing divisions

- **Relationship manager.** Typically salary and bonus, not an equity owner or minority equity owner. Works directly with smaller clients of the practice—product and service divisions

- **Business manager (COO).** Can be a partner or an employee of the practice (salary and bonus) that coordinates all four divisions. Resolves team conflicts, serves as controller, and provides measurement of results based on individual team members' job descriptions—HR division

- **Specialist.** Can be an internal or external member of the team, or a partner. Specialists offer a specific expertise that contributes to the team wealth management offering. Examples could include intergenerational planning, insurance, lending, financial planning, and trusts—product division

- **Next generation.** Next generation planning of affluent clients. Typically a younger advisor or relationship manager—product and service divisions

- **Investments—analyst position.** Portfolio analysis, investment management, research—product division

- **Business development.** Typically a partner, although she can have a minority equity position. Sole responsibility is the implementation of the marketing division acquisition strategies and the management and development of the team's pipeline—marketing division

- **Registered client associate.** Works with the core affluent clients and delivers loyal client service—service division

- **Administrative assistant.** Supports the partners and client associates through operations. Runs reports, prepares and schedules reviews, provides pitch books, etc.—service division

- **Investment associate.** Role is between senior client associate and financial advisor—service division

- **Planner.** Provides planning for core affluent clients. Takes discovery information and inputs into plan, reviews plans with clients, and brings in specialists as needed. Responsible for coordinating increased penetration of each client, working toward 100 percent wallet share—product division

- **Marketing manager.** Develops branding for team on website, social media, event logistics and follow through, helps team develop and incorporate value proposition, develops and maintains marketing materials and pitch books, organizes client board meetings and networking events. This can be a part-time or full-time employee—marketing division

- **Concierge manager.** Creates Wow moments for clients and maintains special touches throughout the year, maintains client profiles, and makes sure every core affluent client is invited to events they are interested in. Coordinates client appreciation events and fun activities for clients' children—service division

THE RELATIONSHIP MANAGER ROLE

One of the observations I have made that applies to many financial advisors is that they overservice their smaller clients at the expense of their best clients. This dynamic is the result of advisors and their teams wanting to be responsive to all of the clients they are responsible for *and* spend time with the clients that demand the most. However, the consequence of this dynamic is that there is never enough time to lavish more attention on the best clients, losing significant opportunity for additional business and assets. When I point this dynamic out to the many advisory teams that are guilty of it, one of the most common responses is *"I know what you are saying is true but . . ."*

- They were one of my first clients
- They are a neighbor, a friend, a church member, a relative
- They were referred to me by a larger client
- They are related to a larger client
- They are a CPA or attorney that refers clients to me

All of these are valid reasons, but it doesn't solve the problem and it keeps an advisory team from being as productive as they can be.

The solution to this common challenge is to establish a relationship manager (RM) role on the team. It is a recommendation that I make to many teams, and those that have embraced it are amazed by the difference it makes.

As I stated earlier in this chapter, one of the big three essential activities for FAs is contact with their top fifty to seventy-five client relationships—I recommend monthly face or voice contact. Typically, if each FA team member has more than fifty client relationships they are responsible for, the team should add a RM role to work directly with the excess, smaller client relationships. For example, if a team with two financial advisors has a total of two hundred client relationships, each FA would keep fifty of their top relationships, and assign the other hundred to a RM who would report directly to the FAs.

RM ROLES AND RESPONSIBILITIES

Each RM should be able to handle a hundred to 150 clients, with a maximum assignment of 150. The RM would in effect be a clone of the FA partner who assigned the client relationships to the RM. The relationship manager would not develop the wealth management and investment process for their assigned clients but would implement the same process that the FA who worked with the client provided. They would provide investment advice, proactive contact, and oversee the servicing of their assigned clients.

The RM is not the architect but the implementer. They have to be very familiar and comfortable with the team's established processes and be routinely updated on investment strategy changes. They make tactical portfolio and asset allocation changes, update financial plans, and implement planning action steps. They provide market updates, share the team's outlook, and provide their assigned clients with newsworthy items that would affect the clients' accounts. In effect, they manage the assigned clients' portfolios as if it were the FA partner.

A best practice is for the FA partner to be part of the annual review together with the RM, depending on the size and value of the client relationship—focusing on the larger clients assigned to the RM. The RM would schedule and do all the preparation work for the annual review. Additionally, the relationship manager would implement all the action steps that would come as a result of the review and the necessary documentation. The FA would typically spend thirty minutes or less on each of these annual reviews, with the RM spending the additional time with the client during the review if needed.

The RM works with FA partners to determine the contact frequency of the RM's assigned relationships. It is appropriate to tier the contacts to the size and priority of the assigned clients. As an example, the highest priority clients assigned to them would be contacted six times a year (including a semiannual and annual review), while a lower priority client might be assigned quarterly contact. Additionally, the RM oversees any service issues associated with the assigned clients and when necessary does the service work. The RM completes all the documentation relating to contact and reviews of assigned clients.

TRANSITIONING CLIENTS TO A RELATIONSHIP MANAGER

One of the biggest challenges that FA partners face when adding a relationship manager is transitioning second-tier clients to the RM. I recommend that the financial advisor personally have the transition conversation—with the RM on the call—with affected clients. The conversation should include the following points:

- The FA has added a partner to help ease the capacity constraints of the practice.
- The FA has not been able to provide the service the client is entitled to and as a result is assigning the client to the RM.
- The FA will provide the RM's background and why the FA is comfortable with this assignment.
- The RM will be implementing the same wealth management and investment process, with FA oversight.
- The FA will be available if needed.
- The FA will continue to be part of the annual reviews.

If the client objects the FA has a decision to make:

- The FA can continue to work with the client (the least desirable option).

- The FA can ask the client to give it a try for ninety days before deciding.
- The FA can tell the client if that's not acceptable the FA will assign the client to another advisory team that has more capacity.

Relationship Manager Transition Script

The following script summarizes the above points:

> *Mr./Ms. Client, I have done an assessment of my practice and am committed to providing a high level of service to all my clients. To help me achieve our service commitment last year I brought on a team member, [name of RM]. I have assigned [name of RM] to cover your account with my oversight to ensure you have the attention you deserve and I have complete confidence that [name] will do an excellent job in servicing your accounts. I wanted to personally introduce you to [name of RM], who is also on the call. I will continue to be involved with your account and am committed to meeting with you at least once a year.*

Note: This client transition process to the new RM should take approximately four to five weeks. It could take up to six months to transition a hundred clients to a new RM.

RM Qualifications

The best relationship managers have different characteristics than the best financial advisors. The primary difference is that they don't possess the desire (or possibly the ability) to acquire new affluent clients. For a financial advisor, this is an essential characteristic.

The RM should be personable, professional, have good impact and communication skills, and have strong organizational skills. She should be service-oriented and confidant but not overly ambitious (another difference from a financial advisor).

RM Background

In searching for a relationship manager, you should consider candidates that have the following backgrounds:

- Registered and experienced client associate
- Financial advisor who has not been successful in bringing in new affluent clients
- Mid-level CPA—not a partner
- Mid-level or junior attorney—not a partner
- Financial planner
- Undergraduate with a business degree, or an MBA with some business experience
- Former teacher—former teachers can make excellent relationship managers

Note: being registered before becoming a RM is a requirement, although you can hire a relationship manager with the expectation that he will become registered before assuming that role.

This is by no means an exclusive list—it should provide you with some ideas of where to source your RM.

RM Compensation

The compensation range for a RM should be $75,000 to $120,000. There may be some exceptions on either side of that range depending on your location, with the West Coast and Northeast being on the higher end of that range. It is important to make sure your RM's compensation expectations are realistic. RMs are not likely to make more than $120,000, with very incremental raises after that level. The people in our industry that make more than that are FAs who are capable of bringing in new million-dollar clients, which is not part of the RM's job description. If the RM wants to make more than the stated range she must be willing to acquire new affluent clients; in that case she would be considered an FA and a new RM would be hired.

Typically, the RM position is a salary and bonus position which does not have equity ownership in the practice. However, if the team leadership decides to pay an RM as an FA, it should be a very small percentage. For example, if an FA team were doing $2 million in business the RM could be paid as a 10 percent partner instead of a salary and bonus. The risk would be if the team substantially grows their practice, the RM could easily exceed the $120,000 compensation limit.

I'm often asked if the cost of an RM is worth it. Here's a story I like to share that explains why I believe the cost is always justified. I once coached an FA who had a very successful practice but was overwhelmed by the number of clients he had. Fred was doing $2 million and wanted to take his practice to the next level with a goal of $3 million in the near future. In analyzing his practice, it was obvious to me he had too many clients to manage. I told him he needed to divest 100 to 150 of his smaller relationships. He refused to take my advice because he felt too close to all of his clients and believed he had a personal obligation to them. As an alternative, I suggested adding an RM to his team. We found Tom, an FA in his office who was in his third year and had his CFP but was a lower producer and was not good at acquiring new affluent clients. My client approached Tom and offered him the RM role at $100,000, which was actually a pay raise for him. He accepted the offer and the FA gave him 120 of his client relationships. The vast majority of the clients accepted the transition to the RM and Tom took over responsibility for their accounts. The end result was that Fred's business grew by 15 percent the next year. He felt his smaller clients were taken care of and the quality of his life was improved—a win-win situation. In his case, he paid the RM 10 percent of his production and gave up $200,000 in production—however his production grew by $400,000 because he had more time to spend with his best clients and more time for business acquisition.

By transitioning smaller clients to a relationship manager, FA partners have more time to spend with their best clients—increasing wallet share and having more time for business development. In the meantime, the RM will most likely produce more from the smaller clients they serve, since they are spending more time with those clients than you would have been able to.

RM ACCOUNTABILITY

The RM should be held accountable for the following tasks:

➤ Strong service experience the team's clients have come to expect

➤ Number of contacts made during the year

➤ Client retention

➤ Expansion of wallet share of assigned clients

➤ Adherence to investment strategy provided by FA partners

TEAM BEST PRACTICES ROLES AND RESPONSIBILITIES CHECKLIST

There are many variables to consider in determining what roles and responsibilities are needed and how to assign them. It takes time and thought, but without the right people doing the right things a team will never reach the highly functioning stage.

❑ Does your team have clearly defined roles and responsibilities?

❑ Do the FA partners spend the majority of their time doing big three, $500/hour work?

❑ Do you have written job descriptions for every team member?

- ❏ Have you assigned three to five high-priority jobs that are measurable to each team member?
- ❏ Have you considered adding a relationship manager to the team?
- ❏ Has your team divided roles and responsibilities into the four divisions?

5

Performance Reviews and Measurements

One of my mentors, Larry Biederman, a former regional manager at Merrill Lynch, once told me, "*You can't manage anything you can't measure.*" It was one of the best pieces of advice that I ever received.

While creating roles and responsibilities is an essential team best practice, without measuring the performance of those roles and responsibilities you will not have a real handle on whether or not your team is working to its highest capacity.

To implement the performance team best practices, start with the codified roles and responsibilities that you assigned each team member. Each job description must have a measurable component. Ask yourself, "Which tasks are measurable?" and "What are the most important aspects of the job to measure?" If you can't measure an activity or a goal than the team member can't be held accountable for their work. If each job has too many measurables, the job itself becomes overwhelming. As a rule of thumb, team members are much more productive in performing fewer high-priority tasks really well than many tasks at a mediocre level.

MEASURABLE ACTIVITIES AND GOALS

When we coach advisors on performance measurement we tell them to assign three to five high-priority tasks with measurable goals to each team member. That doesn't mean that they are limited to only these tasks and goals; these are the areas that they will be evaluated on for their bonuses and raises. The other tasks are basic requirements of the job and it is expected that they will be done well. An example of a basic job requirement for an administrative assistant would be answering the phone in a professional manner or ensuring that a new client is properly entered into the system and making sure all the needed paperwork is processed. A performance task that is measurable might be "implementing Wow touches for top fifty clients." Both performance tasks and basic job requirements should be listed in the job description.

Next, make sure that performance monitoring is measurable. For example, if a team has an administrative assistant, the job description might include "client service." While that is the appropriate job of an administrative assistant, it's hard to measure client service: It lacks definition and covers too broad an area of responsibility. Instead, the job descriptions should break down the tasks of client service and determine what is measurable and what's most important to measure. Measurable tasks could include any of the following—but remember, you will only assign and measure three to five of the highest priority tasks to each team member. (When in doubt, fewer tasks is better)

- Effectively screening calls—following the script when screening nonessential calls for the FAs, so the FAs can focus on their best clients and prospective clients
- Resolving problems for the team's top one hundred clients within forty-eight hours—elevating more difficult problems to the next level
- Setting up client reviews in advance to include agenda items, quarterly and annual results, notes from the last review, handouts
- Implementing the onboarding checklist for new clients
- Competing client profile forms for personal information on team's clients in the first quarter

- Creating and executing Wow touches for team's top one hundred clients
- Setting up and implementing client anniversary acknowledgements
- Setting up logistics for all client and prospect events

Another typical job description is "business development." In this case the activities are just as important as results. The following measurable job descriptions would be assigned to the FA partner who is responsible for business development for the team (or spread between all the FA partners if one doesn't have that primary responsibility):

- Four referral conversations a month
- Meet with five new CPAs each quarter
- One appointment with a million-dollar prospect each week, or four a month
- Build the pipeline of million-dollar prospects to twenty-five
- Acquire $20 million in assets from new clients in a given year

PERFORMANCE RATINGS

One of the biggest challenges that financial advisory teams face is not aligning roles and responsibility with thoughtful performance reporting and reviews. I spent over twenty years as a manager at Merrill Lynch and I was always impressed by how simply and effectively they managed my performance. Every year my manager would assign me new "CFOs"—critical few objectives. There were typically five CFOs each year; my performance was evaluated and my compensation based on the successful completion of those objectives. It was clear to me and to the organization that the basics of my job—adhering to the compliance and HR policies, being responsive to my constituents (FAs and clients), and maintaining good morale in my office—were the reasons I got to keep my job. However, my compensation was based on how I performed on the CFOs.

Again, Merrill Lynch made it very simple and assigned four potential ratings for each of the CFOs:

- **FE.** Far exceeds requirements
- **ER.** Exceeds requirements
- **MR.** Meets requirements
- **DNM.** Does not meet requirements

It was made clear at the beginning of every year what the measurable requirements were for each of my CFOs. These measurables were tracked monthly so I always knew where I stood relative to the performance expectations. I was given a mid-year review by my manager that was designed to be developmental to ensure I would get the highest rating possible, and an annual review where my final rating was assigned and reviewed with my manager. At the end of the year I was given a final rating that took into account my overall success in completing or attending to the CFOs.

This simple performance evaluation process was so effective that in coaching teams to measure performance I use the same process with the teams I consult. The following is an example:

Roles and Responsibility—Client Service— Administrative Associate

High-Priority Measurables (CFOs)

1. Set up client reviews in advance to include agenda items, quarterly and annual results, notes from the last review, handouts
2. Implement the onboarding checklist for new clients
3. Complete client profile form for personal information on team's clients in the first quarter

4. Create and execute Wow touches for team's top hundred clients

5. Set up logistics for all client and prospect events

The ratings assigned should be based on objective criteria that are shared with the employee. Each task or goal should have a clearly codified rating scale. For example, the following would work for the task of client reviews:

- **FE.** Reviews are prepared in advance of the meetings and always complete; the associate always follows up on all the action steps as the result of the review.
- **ER.** Reviews were always prepared in advance of the meetings and always complete.
- **MR.** Reviews were prepared most of the time in advance of the meetings and were complete.
- **DNM.** Reviews were not prepared consistently in advance of meeting and were incomplete.

Sample Ratings

There always should be some subjectivity that is part of the evaluation process—such as a positive attitude, client compliments, "can do" attitude, etc. But the primary factor in performance evaluations should be the objective measures. For example, a performance review rating might look like this:

1. Client reviews—ER
2. Onboarding—ER
3. Client Wow moments—FE
4. Complete and update client profiles—ER
5. Events—MR
6. Overall rating—ER

Assign a Controller

A senior member of the team—typically an FA partner or a senior associate—needs to assume the role of the controller. In a horizontal team the role of the controller can be rotated, but doesn't have to be; typically it's not.

The controller monitors the three to five high-priority measurables assigned to each team member and measures the results and activities of each. Some of these goals can be self-reported results through activities, while others are observations that may not be apparent on the firm's internal reports. It's the controller's responsibility to gather the information, compare the results with the goals and activities, and assign a rating for each based on the comparison. The final report provided by the controller should be done in advance of the semiannual and annual reviews. Then, either the team review committee or the team member who is responsible for that employee participates in the evaluation process and weighs in on the final review rating.

Create a Strict Review Process

I have seen that employees would rather have a review with negative feedback than the ambiguity of no reviews or feedback. The majority of best practicing teams conduct employee reviews twice a year, with both a mid-year and annual review. A few of the best practicing teams did quarterly reviews, and a few did only annual reviews. In my experience, a semiannual review schedule is optimal—it keeps employees appraised of their performance but it's not overwhelming for the team to administer. I would also encourage spontaneous informal feedback throughout the year as opportunities occur. A typical mid-year review can last thirty minutes, and an annual review thirty to sixty minutes.

The annual and mid-year reviews should focus on seven primary areas:

1. Team members' input
2. Observed behavior by controller and assigned FA or senior client associate
3. Individual's self-assessment
4. Team commitment (were they a team player?)
5. Positive attitude
6. Client feedback
7. Results compared to the three to five clearly defined performance goals and activities

Additionally, the annual review would include any adjustment of roles and responsibilities and performance goals from the mid-year review, if needed. The annual review features a final rating which determines year-end compensation administered through raises, bonuses, and pool splits, depending on the role of the employee.

COMPENSATION REVIEWS ARE WORTH THE TIME THEY TAKE

Setting up a good performance measurement and review process takes time, but it is essential to having a highly functioning team. Developing this process should be done as a high priority once the team has formed.

Sample Performance Review

The following is a template that can be used for mid-year and annual reviews. The mid-year review will focus more on tracking the performance of the three to five high-priority performance goals, while the annual review encompasses most if not all of these review items.

The first part of the review focuses on the team's assessment of the individual:

- Review of results compared to three to five high-priority per-
  formance goals and activities
- Team members' input
- Observed behavior by controller and FA they are assigned to
  or senior client associate
- Team commitment
- Positive attitude
- Client feedback

The second part of the review can be the individual's self-assessment. You can provide some combination of these questions in
advance, or ask them during the review:

- What are your contributions to the team?
- What are some things that could have gone better in your job?
- Are there areas that you would like to develop?
- Is there anything you would change or do differently?
- Are there things you would like to do more or less of?
- Do you feel the roles, responsibilities, and goals feel right?
- What do you enjoy doing in your job?
- Is there anything you wish you didn't have to do?
- Is there anything that I need to do differently?
- Are there any areas you think the team could improve on?

FA Reviews

Best practicing teams review the financial advisor partners, including
the senior partners. I have found in coaching financial advisors that
accountability is a powerful driver of positive behavior: If the team
is serious about improving its productivity, accountability should be
present at all levels. The FA partners in best practicing teams hold
each other accountable to even higher performance levels than
the non-FA members of the team. Typically, senior partners review
junior partners, and senior partners review each other. The senior

partner review makes sure that the partners are holding each other accountable in a positive way; accountability is a powerful driver of human behavior.

Examples of high-priority goals and activities (but not an all-inclusive list) that FA partners could be accountable for include:

- Business development activities—number of referral conversations, client CPA meetings, million-dollar prospect meetings, hosting prospect events
- Client contact—monthly contact of top fifty clients and quarterly reviews
- Community involvement—local or national nonprofit board membership
- Client service—random acts of kindness examples, attendance at client life events, meeting clients' children, intergenerational planning meetings
- Business increase with assigned clients
- Wallet share increase with assigned clients
- Financial plans executed and updated with assigned clients
- Continuing education—professional associations, professional designations, development of specialization or expertise
- Team meetings attended, employee reviews administered, time spent mentoring and training new hires or junior team members

A team is only as strong as its weakest link. Performance reviews provide the team the opportunity to recognize strong performance, improve average performance, and drop poor performers from the team. Performance reporting and reviews take time, but the return on investment can be increased productivity, higher morale, and the loyalty of high-performing team members.

The final component of accountability is fair compensation based on performance, which will be covered in the next chapter.

PERFORMANCE MEASUREMENT TEAM BEST PRACTICES CHECKLIST

❏ Have you taken each job description and assigned how performance can be measured in three to five of the highest-priority jobs?

❏ Have you set goals for each team member that define the difference between unacceptable, acceptable, and excellent levels of performance?

❏ Have you set up periodic performance reviews? What is their frequency?

❏ Have you written what each performance review will cover?

❏ Have you assigned a team member as controller to track activities and results of team members' job descriptions and goals?

6

Team Compensation

R oles and responsibilities, performance measurements, and compensation are the cornerstones of accountability. All three of these best practices are tied together; without one the others don't mean very much. The highest-functioning teams understand the importance of accountability and have incorporated it into their team best practices.

Compensation is the tangible reward for a job well done. As important as clearly defined roles and responsibilities and performance measurements are, without fair compensation they won't drive behavior or engender loyalty. All the best practicing teams understand that loyalty and job satisfaction are essential to their overall success: Generous and fair compensation is the best way to keep team members wanting to provide superior service to their clients.

COMPENSATION GUIDELINES: WHAT CAN AND CAN'T BE REWARDED

The team should make every attempt to ensure that compensation is fair. The best way to ensure fairness is to have compensation based on clearly defined roles and responsibilities that are tied to objective and consistent performance reviews. Too often, compensation for a financial advisory team's members is based on subjective decisions that can't be defended and reviews are never conducted. Or worse, below-average team members are overcompensated.

The expression "fair but not equal" should be a compensation policy embraced by teams. I believe the best-performing team members should be compensated generously, and the average and lower-performing team members should not be. The key is for all the team members to know the difference between high, average, and low performance. By using the review process in Chapter 4, all team members can be on the same page regarding what is expected of them.

The next step is to link performance to compensation. In developing a compensation plan for the team, several factors should be taken into account. The team must be aware of what their highest priorities are and make sure that compensation reflects those priorities. Examples of high priorities could include:

- Business growth
- New assets acquired
- Raving fan clients
- World-class service
- World-class wealth management offering

The team has to take the next step and identify measurable goals and activities associated with each of these high priorities. Then, compensation can be based on the performance of these activities.

Some performance goals are well within the control of each team member, and these are the goals that can be tied to compensation. Controllable goals could include:

- Client satisfaction scores on surveys
- Client review preparation
- Implementation of Wow touches
- Positive attitude
- Problem resolution
- Prospect meetings
- Random acts of kindness (numbers of them)
- Referral conversations

However, some aspects of job performance rely on external factors, including the financial markets, or on the performance of other team members. These factors should not be taken into consideration when reviewing team members or determining their compensation. Examples might include:

- Market performance
- Short-term portfolio returns
- Overall team revenue
- Client turnover
- Cash outflows

SUPPORT STAFF COMPENSATION STRUCTURE

There are three elements of compensation that the majority of the highest-functioning teams use for their support staff. These include the base salary, annual individual performance bonus, and annual team performance bonus.

Support Staff Base Salary

The support staff base salary is tagged to the market value of each team member's position. Most teams have very little control of how much their firm is willing to pay a nonproducer or administrative position. In most cases to attract and retain a good performer the team must be willing to supplement the firm's base salary. The supplemental salary is required to attract, retain, and reward loyalty. It should also be noted that once a supplemental salary is provided it shouldn't be lowered: It is typically a fixed percent of the team's total business. The combination of the firm's base and the team's supplemental salary then becomes the support staff base salary.

In interviewing best practicing teams, the majority paid supplemental compensation in the range of 0.5 to 2 percent of total business generated the previous year to each non-producing team member—the percentage would be based on seniority and the scope of responsibility of each role. It is important to note that in high-cost living areas like the Northeast and West Coast the firm base salary and supplemental salary would be on the higher end of the range, and in some cases even exceed it.

As some teams are moving to independent and RIA models, the base portion of the firm's support salary is paid by the partners in the team. The base salary must be established as one that is competitive enough to attract and retain loyal, high-performing employees. In addition, supplemental compensation is given for satisfactory job performance. If overall job performance is not satisfactory, the employee should be put on probation; if improvement is not made by the next mid-year review, the employee might be terminated.

Here's an example: If a team produced $2 million in revenues and paid 1 percent in the form of supplemental compensation to each nonproducing team member, they would pay each nonproducing team member an average of $20,000 in supplemental compensation (assuming that for most teams producing at that level they would have at most two nonproducing team members). If the firm salary was $40,000 and the supplemental compensation was $20,000, the nonproducing team member's base salary would be $60,000.

Support Staff Annual Bonus

The annual bonus is the portion of the compensation plan that rewards job performance. The basis for the annual bonus should be controllable, measurable, and a high priority to the team. This portion of compensation is based on the three to five measurable high-priority activities that result in achievement of the team member's goals, as discussed in Chapter 4. Each of these critical few objectives (CFOs) are assigned one of the following ratings: far exceeds requirements (FE), exceeds requirements (ER) meets requirements (MR), does not meet requirements (DNM).

Based on the performance of the CFO ratings, an overall rating is assigned to each team member, and that rating is tied to her year-end or annual bonus. It is acceptable to have a portion of the overall rating be subjective, but this should be a relatively small factor in the final rating. By following this process the team can be assured that they are administering a fair compensation plan.

The annual bonus is not an entitlement, and it must be earned. A team member could be assigned a FE rating one year and a MR rating another, depending on his performance and the CFOs assigned that year. This is what keeps employees working at the highest levels: They do not want to negatively impact their bonus and overall compensation.

The compensation range within each category depends on the size of the team, the seniority of the nonproducing team member, and the number of nonproducing team members on the team. As a general guideline, an overall FE rating should represent a 30 percent increase in the team member's base salary. An ER rating should represent a 20 percent increase and an MR requirement a zero to 10 percent increase.

If the average rating for the team members would be an ER, then the team should budget 20 percent of the total team's base salary toward the team bonus pool. For example, if a team had two administrative assistants with base salaries of $60,000 each, then the partners should budget $24,000 for their annual bonuses ($120,000 total in salaries x 20% = $24,000 bonus pool). If we used the prior example of an administrative assistant who was paid $40,000 by the firm, received $20,000 supplemental compensation, and earned an overall ER rating which paid $12,000—her overall compensation would be $72,000 including the team bonus.

Support Staff Team Performance Bonus

The team performance bonus is paid only to nonproducing team members, and is based on how well the entire team performed.

This bonus should be viewed like an annual profit-sharing plan. If the team does well the bonus pool should be expanded, but in a poor performing year the bonus pool would be contracted (and in a worst-case scenario, could be eliminated). However, the team bonus should be distributed to individual team members based on their performance ratings. For example, if the team has been growing at an average 5 percent annual rate, and that growth rate reaches a 10 percent growth rate one year, then it would be appropriate to provide a team bonus to the non-financial advisors on the team. If all the non-FA employees are assigned high-priority controllable and measurable goals, those who achieve the highest ratings would be the biggest contributors: Their share of the team bonus would be greater than an employee with a lower rating—"Fair but not equal."

The purpose of the team bonus is to motivate individual team members to do all they can to contribute to reaching the team's goals. It also encourages team spirit and individuals working outside their normal responsibilities when needed. With few exceptions, the best practicing teams we worked with had a partner/team bonus pool to encourage team camaraderie.

Examples of team performance bonus:

- **FE**—$3,000 to $5,000
- **ER**—$1,500 to $3,000
- **MR**—zero to $1,000

As a guideline, consider contributing 5 percent of the production growth to the team performance bonus pool. For example, if a $2 million team grew by 10 percent ($200,000) than $10,000 (5 percent) would be allocated to the team performance bonus pool. An administrative assistant whose compensation was $72,000 through base salary and annual performance bonus, and whose performance rating was ER, would earn an additional $2,000 for a total compensation package of $74,000.

There are no guarantees that a team bonus will be paid each year, and it will be entirely dependent on the team reaching or exceeding its annual goals.

Support Staff Raises

At Altius, we suggest giving the support staff small, incremental raises every year to reward loyalty and experience. Typically, annual raises are based on the base salary portion of the overall compensation. The best practicing teams do not rely on big raises to reward the best performers. Rather, they use the annual bonus rating system described. Often the raises are defined by the firm, since the supplemental compensation is based on the production of the team and will automatically be raised as business is increased and lowered when business drops. The result is that annual or cost of living raises constitute a very small portion of a nonproducer's compensation.

RETAINED EARNINGS CONTRIBUTIONS

Team compensation among best practicing teams generally accounts for 75 percent of the annual retained earnings, dollars earned that they put back in their business. Among best practicing teams, this is between 7.5 and 15 percent of the total partner income. For example, if an FA earns $500,000, he would put approximately $50,000 back into the business. And of the $50,000, then $35,000 (75 percent) would go toward team compensation.

For advisors working in the independent and RIA channel, the percentage of income contributed to team compensation would be higher. As a result, the high percentage for this channel must be covered by the FA partners. Independent and RIA channel advisors get a higher percentage payout then the wire houses, so they have more money to put back into their practices because their firms don't provide the same level of financial support in terms of salaries paid to the non-FA team members because of their smaller split of the team's total business.

If a team decides that each partner should contribute 10 percent of their income to the team bonus pools, a junior partner would pay their prorated share, but that number would be much less than the share of a senior partner.

MEET AMANDA

An example that I like to use that explains the financial value of a high-performing, experienced team employee is Amanda, the administrative assistant of my own financial advisor. Amanda joined my advisor's team about twenty years ago and has been working with our family for the majority of that time. The majority of my contact with my advisor's team is with Amanda: She coordinates every aspect of the administrative side of our account. This includes the wiring of money to my children when they need loans from us, ensuring that when they are traveling overseas and need money they are able to get it, detecting and alerting us to fraudulent use of credit cards, reviewing details of our statements, setting up and closing accounts as needed, and handling every administrative issue with all of our accounts. Our family requires a fair amount of handholding, and there is always an administrative task that has to be done. Amanda handles all of these details with a positive attitude. My wife and children love Amanda as well.

From my financial advisor's standpoint, Amanda is a godsend. He never has to deal with any of the administrative details of our account. He only needs to talk to me during our monthly contact when we talk about my investments and my progress toward my financial goal. She enables him to focus on the big three activities as they relate to our accounts. What is the value of Amanda to my advisor? Priceless. He recognizes her value and is very generous with her compensation—an extremely good investment on his part. Amanda makes a six-figure compensation package.

PARTNER/SENIOR FA COMPENSATION STRUCTURE

Partners should be willing to make adjustments to their compensation for the following two reasons:

1. One or more partners exceed individual contribution goals
2. One or more partners falls short of goals

The reason that this practice is important is the partners should be incentivized to do everything they can to improve the performance and productivity of the overall team. If an FA's individual team split is 10 percent of business generated then her ability to significantly impact her compensation is minimal no matter how much she contributes. For example, a team member with a 10 percent split could have a year where his individual production was up 100 percent, but if the rest of the team was flat he would only get a 10 percent raise. The reverse can also happen: If a senior team member receives a relatively high percentage of the team split but is working part-time and not contributing in alignment to her split, then it would be a disincentive for the other team members to work hard and contribute more than their share.

Adjusting the team members' pool splits is also consistent with the succession planning that I described in Chapter 2. As a senior partner transitions out of the business toward retirement, his partnership split would decrease while the remaining partners' would increase.

Some teams have multiple pools that FAs share based on business brought in, but this can be confusing and needs to be simplified as much as possible—with a caution on having too many pool splits.

Best practicing teams keep compensation and pool splits simple to avoid confusion, complication, and a large number of different split arrangements. They hold an annual partners meeting at the end of the year. This meeting is designed to review the additional compensation of each of the partners, and particularly the percentages each received of the overall team pool. During the meeting, each partner has the opportunity to make a case for a split adjustment if they feel a change is warranted. The case should be based on performance as it relates to productive assets brought in and business generated. The senior partners of the team review the case made and determine if an adjustment should be made for the upcoming year. Senior partners must be willing to be reviewed by each other and be open-minded if their split should be increased or decreased.

Typically, FA compensation changes would occur as the result of succession planning or adjustments made to give junior partners a higher split. Harold, one of the senior members of a top-performing team, has consistently given up a share of his split to younger members of the team as he works less and they work more.

The annual partner's compensation meeting is also the time to review the succession plan and ensure that the business plan is being followed, and adjustments to compensation and business practices are being made according to the plan.

PARTNER COMPENSATION GUIDELINES

The most successful teams understand the value and importance of attracting and retaining high-performing employees. They recognize that the ROI on a thoughtful compensation plan is very high. By building a strong team with loyal, productive employees, the partners are able to delegate better and focus on the most productive tasks. Retaining their best employees ensures a loyal client base and a growing and productive practice.

On the best practicing teams, the overall FA partners' contributions to team compensation, as I mentioned previously, generally fall into a range of 7.5 to 15 percent of each partner's individual compensation. For example, if a partner in a $5 million team earns $1.2 million in total compensation (40 percent payout is the average for most firms), she would contribute (at 10 percent) $120,000 of her earnings into the team pool.

Top Producers Compensation Example:

☞ **$2 million team.** Partner receives 40 percent payout = $800,000 in compensation. Partner's 10 percent team compensation budget is $80,000

☞ **Nonproducer #1.** $75,000 total compensation. Firm pays $40,000, team pays $35,000 (supplemental base compensation, performance bonus, and team bonus)

☞ **Nonproducer #2.** $80,000 total compensation (higher rating or more experience). Firm pays $40,000, team pays $40,000 (supplemental base compensation, performance bonus, and team bonus)

☞ **Total Team Supplemental Compensation =** $75,000 (within team budget of $80,000)

RECOGNITION BEYOND COMPENSATION

Recognizing members of the team for their good performance is both powerful and relatively cheap, and typically not done enough. However, best practicing teams do it all the time. They understand that compensation without recognition is not enough: High performers like to be appreciated for their efforts. If a fair compensation plan is the cake then recognition is the icing; while either one is good, the combination of both is special.

Every partner on the team should be encouraged to look for ways to recognize good performance—awareness is the key. There are so many ways that senior members or partners of a team can provide recognition. Examples of some of the team best practices include:

- Recognizing employees at team meetings with a compliment or an example or a story of how a team member provided a client with outstanding service
- Providing a small gift card for solving a key client problem
- Sending flowers on the employee's service anniversary or birthday
- Giving a gift certificate to a nice restaurant for a junior partner bringing in a new affluent client
- Writing a nice handwritten note for planning and handling the logistics of a successful client or prospect event
- Organizing a team dinner or weekend trip for all team members for reaching a milestone goal
- Privately thanking a team member for a job well done
- Sending an email to other team members about a particular member's job well done
- Sharing examples of outstanding work during performance reviews

COMPENSATION TEAM BEST PRACTICES CHECKLIST

- ❏ Is your non-producer team's compensation based on factors within each team member's control?
- ❏ Is your non-producer team compensation based on a manageable number of high-priority goals and activities?
- ❏ Does your nonproducer compensation include base salary, individual performance bonuses, and team performance bonuses?

❑ Is the individual performance bonus of nonproducing team members tied to a performance measurement process that includes semiannual reviews and an objective rating system?

❑ Are the best-performing team members paid in the top 25 percent of their peers with the same job description and experience level?

❑ Does the team have an annual partner's compensation meeting where team pool splits can be adjusted as needed?

❑ Does the team have a budget for supplemental team compensation typically between 7.5 and 15 percent of the team's earnings (double for independent and RIA channel teams)?

❑ Is recognition for high performance part of the team's culture and encouraged?

7

Team Communication

est practicing teams communicate frequently and consistently because they know that communication is necessary for the team to function optimally. When motivated and talented individuals who share the same priorities and are working on common goals communicate frequently, good things happen. If a team excels, good and consistent communication exists, and when a team fails it can always be traced back to poor communication.

I remember as a sole practitioner I "was lonely in my own head." If I was stuck on a problem, had a prospect or client challenge, or experienced a setback, I struggled to come up with solutions because I only had myself to rely on. Once I was part of a team I could brainstorm with other team members who I respected and who had the same goals. I knew that each team member offered a different perspective; once a course of action was determined it was validated by the other team members, which gave me more confidence in my decisions.

There are seven primary reasons that best practicing teams have frequent and consistent internal communication:

1. It ensures all team members are aware of the team's vision and business plan, and keeps that vision in their thoughts on a consistent basis.
2. It enables all team members to provide input and ideas on how to help the team continually improve.
3. It ensures that all team members are on the same page, communicating the same message to clients and prospects.

4. It helps the team overcome challenges by having multiple points of view on potential solutions.
5. It enables team members to ensure that everyone is working on getting their job done, and that delegation and follow up aren't falling through the cracks.
6. It provides the team confidence that decisions are made and good solutions provided because they have been vetted by multiple and committed team members.
7. It provides accountability to the team partners for reaching their production, new asset, and new affluent client goals.

COMMUNICATION MEANS MEETINGS

In my experience with highly functioning teams, there are a few types of meetings teams need to hold on a regular basis. Meetings offer a forum for team communication.

Daily Meetings

These meetings are short and done at the same time every day—typically, first thing in the morning. They are designed to address the specific challenges of that day. They are also designed to review the calendar for that day: client reviews, events, prospect meetings, and office meetings. The daily meeting is also an opportunity for partners to delegate tasks to nonproducing team members and to get updated on past high-priority tasks that they have delegated. It is the ideal time for the FA team members so assign $30/hour tasks to administrative team members so they can focus on the $500/hour big three activities throughout the day.

Daily meetings are commonly called "stand up" meetings to send the message that there is not time to sit down—they are tactical and fast. These meetings typically last no more than ten or fifteen minutes. If they last longer than fifteen minutes they become burdensome, and people lose interest in making this daily commitment.

Weekly Meetings

These meetings are the cornerstone for team communication and are something that all the best practicing teams I have worked with do consistently. We recommend that weekly team meetings are done on the same day, at the same time, and that all team members participate. I strongly recommend the weekly team meetings last no longer than an hour.

Weekly meetings are of paramount importance. They are not skipped or postponed as long as at least two senior team members or partners are present. For the weekly team meetings to be effective they must be a high priority and the senior team members must be committed to them. At Altius we have noticed that teams, however well intentioned, that don't maintain the discipline needed to conduct meetings every week do not function as well as those teams that do.

We recommend holding weekly meetings on Monday afternoons. By having them on Monday the team has a clear direction for the week, has outlined the weekly priorities, and has reviewed the weekly calendar. Another reason that Monday is a good day for the team meeting is that typically all team members are at work on Mondays, ensuring good attendance. We strongly recommend having a written agenda for the weekly team meeting, and it should be followed closely.

Typical Weekly Meeting Topics

The weekly team meeting is really the cornerstone of team communication, and much can be accomplished if the right topics are covered the right way. While the highest-functioning teams held meetings with different agendas, they typically cover the same topics.

In allocating time for the following agenda items, the person in charge of creating the weekly agenda must organize it so that the meeting will run for no more than an hour. That means that some agenda items may have to be eliminated and others expanded as needed. The following should be viewed as a menu from which topics are chosen, with the idea that each of these items is covered *at least* once a month. For example, when the prospect pipeline is reviewed, perhaps the market review is not covered that week; when monthly results are covered or acquisition strategies reviewed, then service or business ideas might not be featured.

- **Calendar.** A review of last week's calendar to discuss successes, loose ends, lessons learned. Also, a review of the upcoming week's calendar including preparation needed, events scheduled, and desired outcomes. Additionally, a review of the ninety-day calendar and any action that needs to be taken, including coverage for anticipated vacations, holidays, or maternity leave. Approximate time allocation—10 minutes.

- **Market Review.** The investment committee reports on asset allocation changes, model portfolio review, strategy changes, market updates, money managers or asset managers to be put on watch list, removed, or added. This topic may not be covered every week if the investment committee has not met or no significant changes occur. Approximate time allocation—10 minutes, twice a month.

- **Business Ideas.** This can be driven by the market review if a specific investment idea or asset manager is featured. In some cases, a major campaign could be suggested and launched if a significant opportunity presents itself. A best practice could be that each FA takes turns and shares a business idea that they are excited about. Approximate time allocation—10 minutes.

- **Client Review.** A specific top fifty client is featured where the FA assigned to that client provides the rest of the team a profile of that client so that each team member has an in-depth knowledge of the team's best clients, even if they are not assigned to them. This is especially helpful for the client associates. It could also include a review of a new client brought in. Typically one client is featured and time allocated to this is no more than 5 minutes.

- **Service.** This topic should be driven by the administrative managers and associates, and should cover service issues, challenges, and suggestions. It should include updates on service initiatives put in place and resolution of any significant outstanding service issues the team might have. It is also an opportunity to share "random acts of kindness" that were delivered, and a review of top fifty client birthdays or other significant happenings in the best clients' lives. Approximate time allocation—10 minutes.

- **Results.** This is when the team controller (an existing team member—this is an ancillary role in addition to her primary role) reports results versus goals. This can be an expanded agenda item once a month, where business, new assets, and new affluent client households are tracked versus goals set. Every week it can be an opportunity to highlight any significant wins that occurred, and the FA team members can share these wins with the rest of the team. Time allocated—if monthly, 15 minutes; if weekly, 5 minutes.

- **Acquisition Strategy Review.** What acquisition strategies are we focused on? Who are we going to apply those strategies to? This meeting topic should occur once or twice a month. Time allocated—15 minutes.

- **Prospect Pipeline.** This is a quick review of the prospect pipeline: Each FA assigned to a prospect gives a quick update and if needed asks for suggestions from rest of the team on ideas about how to stay relevant or close a prospect. This is a formal review once a month. Time allocated—15 minutes.

- **Recognition.** This is an opportunity for team members to recognize outstanding work and results. The team controller has an important role during this time of the meeting, as he knows what results have come in and can provide appropriate recognition. Time allocated—5 minutes.

- **Summary.** The team leader or FA responsible for the meeting closes by asking, "Anything else we need to address that hasn't been covered?" Then he or she does a quick summary and a call to action on the highest priority items. The summary is an opportunity to provide an inspirational message if appropriate. Time allocated—5 minutes.

MARKETING MEETING ADJUSTMENTS

In the marketing division chapter, it is recommended that the team have a separate marketing meeting once or twice a month. For these meetings, the acquisition agenda items could be pulled out of the weekly team meeting and covered during the marketing meeting.

The following sample agenda template can be covered in an hour or less if there is a person responsible for monitoring the time and keep the meeting on track.

WEEKLY MEETING TOPICS

1. Calendar*
   a. Review last week's calendar—any loose ends
   b. Review this week's calendar—what preparation needs to be done

    c. Review 90-day calendar—anticipate vacations, holidays

    d. Upcoming events

2. Market Review

    a. Any changes needed to be made based on current market conditions

    b. Review of mortgage and lending rates

3. Business Ideas*

    a. Sharing of business ideas that could generate business for the week

    b. Reinforce strategy and investment themes

    c. Review money coming available

4. Results*

    a. Tracking compared to goals

    b. Recognize individual accomplishments

    c. Celebrate wins

5. Client Review

    a. Feature a client

    b. Who do we need to know better—clients

    c. Kids of clients that we need to know better

    d. Review of any new client relationship

6. Service

    a. Random acts of kindness examples

    b. Service issues, challenges, ideas

    c. Review birthdays, special occasions

7. Prospect Pipeline (optional—could be covered in marketing meeting)

    a. Review current pipeline

    b. When next contact, who will contact

    c. New prospects added

8. Summary*

    a. Anything else?

    b. Team leader summarizes, inspires, call to action

    *Essential items to cover

Strategic Meetings

These meetings are designed to focus on the big picture and on strategic initiatives of the team. They are much less tactical than either daily or weekly meetings. Most of the best practicing teams conduct these meetings semiannually, but all of them have strategic meetings at least once a year.

Strategic meetings are designed to fulfill the team vision through the implementation of the business plan. This is when the team will set the goals for the year, establish the highest priorities, determine the hiring needs, and establish budgets, including the bonus pools. They review what the team has done best lately, and what the needed areas for improvement are. The most important question that should be asked during the strategic meeting is "How can we get better?" It's the small incremental improvements that a team makes over time that will help them become a world-class operation. It's also an ideal time for recognizing team members who have done outstanding work. Strategic team meetings should be done offsite. As a guideline, the mid-year meeting should be a half day long, and the annual meeting a full day.

I have included a written agenda for these meetings that incorporates the agenda items that the majority of the best teams use.

ANNUAL AND MID-YEAR STRATEGY MEETING AGENDA

1. Business Plan Review and Update

2. Goals and Results

3. Service Model—how can we make it better?

    a. Administrative and operations processes

    b. Wow moments

    c. How can we improve?

4. Acquisition Strategies

    a. Pipeline review

    b. Acquisition goals

5. Investment Committee Forecast and Strategy for Next Year

6. Resources

    a. Additional team members

    b. Budget for upcoming year

7. Calendar of Events for the Year

8. What Can We Do Better?

9. Biggest Wins and Losses

    a. What can we learn?

10. Client Review

    a. Any we need to move?

    b. Any we need to focus on?

    c. Identify highest potential clients

11. Highest Priorities

12. Recognition

Investment Committee Meetings

Many of the best practicing teams I interviewed had monthly investment committee meetings. These meetings were designed to determine and review the policy and strategy of the team's investment management. The meeting is typically attended by the senior partners and the investment analyst (if the team has this position) to review current asset allocation, strategic investment changes, asset manager changes, overall performance of the core portfolios, and investment ideas that need to be communicated to other team members. The notes from the meeting are reviewed with the entire team during the weekly team meeting. These investment committee meetings are typically an hour long.

HOW TO CONDUCT A MEETING

There is nothing more powerful and productive than an effective team meeting—and there is no greater waste of time than an ineffective meeting. When meetings are not well-organized, they drift and run over the time allotted. Sometimes, too much time is spent on informal, irrelevant topics. Or the meeting is poorly attended and then postponed or discontinued because it is a waste of time.

The best practicing teams have established the following principles to conduct impactful, tight, and productive meetings:

1. They have a formal written agenda and stick to it.
2. They designate a senior partner to be the "sergeant at arms" who keeps the meeting on track and keeps team members from wandering off on tangents.
3. There is a time limit for each agenda item and for the overall meeting.
4. An administrative team member asks each team member for agenda items in advance of the meeting that they want to make sure are covered. Those items are incorporated into the appropriate agenda and distributed before the meeting.
5. Senior team members alternate responsibility for conducting the team meeting.
6. Each team member is encouraged to contribute and is assigned responsibility for an agenda item. That member

is tasked to update and follow up on assigned tasks from the past meeting.

7. A nonproducing team member takes notes and sends a summary to all team members after the meeting.

As I reflect on my early experience with my team I believe the most valuable best practice that we employed was good internal team communication. My partner and I met every Saturday. Sometimes it was at one of our houses, sometimes it was at the office, sometimes at a restaurant—but we always did it. We didn't have a formal agenda but we always covered the calendar, business ideas, prospecting strategies, and service, and we came up with new ideas for how we could get better.

Teams that do not institute formal internal communication processes in their practice are missing out on one of the great benefits that a team can offer. The best teams communicate consistently, frequently, and in a disciplined way. That doesn't mean that informal communication between team members isn't valuable, but it's not enough—the structure and accountability take internal communication to the next level.

TEAM BEST PRACTICES COMMUNICATION CHECKLIST

- ❑ Does your team have short daily meetings to review high-priority items?
- ❑ Does your team have a regular weekly meeting with an agenda and all team members contributing and participating?
- ❑ Are weekly team notes taken and distributed to all team members?
- ❑ Does your team have an investment committee and does the committee meet regularly?

❑   Does your team have semiannual offsite strategic meetings?

❑   Does your weekly team agenda include the following?

   Calendar review

   Market update

   Business idea exchange

   Results—accountability

   Recognition

   Client review—feature a client, new client relationships

   Service—update, challenges, successes

   Prospect pipeline review

8

Best Practices for Hiring

The single most important decision a team can make is hiring the right people for the right job. When I think of my career as a Merrill Lynch manager and a founding partner of Altius Learning, I can say without question that the successes I have enjoyed have been the result of the good people I have hired. In the end, a team is only as good as the sum of its parts. The most important questions that senior team members can ask themselves is when to hire, who to hire, and what additions does the team need?

Whenever a new member of a team is brought on that member must have professional values that are consistent with the values of the team. In many ways, a financial services team is like a professional marriage. As people who have had long successful marriages will tell you, having similar values is the glue that holds the marriage together. So just like marrying the right person, choosing new team members should be based on having similar and aligned professional values. Examples of professional values include work ethic, service commitment, empathy, collaboration, positive attitude, and ethics.

A LESSON IN HIRING AND FIRING

One of the most important lessons that I learned over the past thirty years of hiring individuals is to be slow to hire and quick to fire. Most financial services teams are not that large to begin with, so hiring a new member can have significant consequences to the daily lives of existing team members. Because of this, I advise implementing a deliberate and thoughtful hiring process.

The highest-functioning teams I interviewed all maintain a good hiring process that includes the following steps:

1. Multiple interviews for each candidate—screenings and then an in-depth interview
2. Interviews by multiple members of the team to get different perspectives
3. Asking for references and following up with those references
4. Focusing on past quantifiable successes

However, no matter how thoughtful and thorough a hiring process is created, there will be mistakes. Hiring mistakes can usually be identified within ninety days of when a new team member starts. While proper training and development is important, if the new team member demonstrates values that are not consistent with the team, his employment should be terminated. The disruptive nature of a poor hire is too high; having a poor performing team member is a decision that shouldn't be put off.

Every new team member should be told that there is a ninety-day probationary policy to determine whether or not the new hire is a good fit, and that policy should be strictly enforced. By letting any new team member know from the beginning what the expectations are there will be no surprises if she doesn't meet expectations, and she will know exactly what the consequences will be.

WHEN TO HIRE

One of the most important decisions that a team can make is when to hire a new team member. The hiring decision will in most cases require a significant financial commitment, but can also provide an impressive return on that investment if done right. Hiring a team member can be a costly decision but an additional good hire who fits the needs of the team always turns out to be a good return on that investment.

In assessing the need to hire an additional team member I recommend going through the following steps:

- Have a written job description for members of the team: Suggest they write their own. The team should then evaluate whether the job descriptions cover all the team's needs. If the current job descriptions cover all or most of the team's needs, then hiring can be delayed.

- Have the FAs keep a log for a week or two of all the non-big three activities that they engage in. FAs should be focused on development and implementation of the team's wealth management process, contacting top fifty client relationships, and business development (prospecting), while everything else should be delegated. Once the FAs have kept the time log the list of non-big three activities should be consolidated into a job description. If there is an existing non-FA team member or members that has the capacity to perform those tasks, then that list should be delegated to that person. If the existing non-FA team members do not have the capacity to handle these additional tasks, then an additional team member needs to be hired. The rationale is clear why that makes financial sense: If the FA team members can delegate $30/hour tasks then they have more time to do $500/hour work, resulting in a $470/hour benefit.

- The team believes that they are capable of taking their practice to a significantly higher level and decides to hire an additional team member to support future growth. A good example of this scenario is a top advisor that I worked with in Atlanta, Henry Camp. Henry and his team wanted to double their business in three years and realized they couldn't support that growth with their existing team members. Henry hired an additional administrative person to support this anticipated growth and his investment paid off as his team reached their goal ahead of schedule.

- The team decides they need a relationship manager to take care of the smaller client relationships of the team, which will give FA team members more capacity to serve their best clients and business-development activities.

- The team decides they need to add an additional FA to fill a need in their succession planning or to fill a gap in their team's offering (such as intergenerational planning, business development, or risk management).

WHO TO HIRE?

The following are options that a team needs to consider when adding a new team member:

Hiring an Experienced FA

This is typically a sole practitioner with an existing practice that the team believes would be additive to their team. This can be a win-win situation because the high-potential FA would be able to have increased administrative support along with the benefit of working with a larger team with more resources. The acquiring team can accelerate their growth rate by adding a high performer to the team. In this case, the team may not have determined they had a need to add an additional team member but since a high-potential FA is available they can capitalize on it by extending an offer to join the team. If the high-potential FA lives up to their expectations, the senior team members recognize the contributions through a generous team pool split.

For instance, Carl was an advisor with twenty-five years of experience who had built a successful practice within a larger office. Over the years he noticed the work habits and early success that Scott was having. Carl had no immediate need to add an additional FA to his team but he was so impressed with Scott that he made him an offer. Today, Carl will tell you that it was the best business decision he ever made. Scott took his business-development skills and leveraged Carl's experience and expertise. Since Scott joined Carl's team the production of the team has tripled, and both readily admit that neither one would be doing as much business individually as they are together; the whole is greater than the sum of the parts. Carl recognized Scott's contribution and made him a 50/50 partner.

Succession Planning

All high-functioning teams have a succession plan in place. The demographics of our industry are such that a significant percentage of advisors are planning on retiring or are retiring soon. The need for succession planning has never been greater. The senior partners on a team need to determine who will take over their practice when they retire. If they don't have a younger FA on the team they should go on an active search to add one. This can be a very attractive option for a less-senior advisor or even a team of younger advisors as they can take over an existing practice.

The following scenario is a clear indicator of the need for succession planning. Doug is sixty-two years old and has built a very successful practice over forty years. He is the only FA member on his team and has already made the decision to retire in the next four years. This decision became the catalyst to search for a younger FA to add to the team who would take over his practice when he retired. He searched and interviewed a number of potential team members until he found Antony. Antony was fifteen years younger and had already built a successful practice. More important, Doug felt that Antony's values were aligned with his, and he possessed what Doug felt was an important skill for the team's future success, business development. Doug offered Antony a position on his team with the plan they would work together for the next four years. Doug also recruited Amelia, a young, high-potential advisor, to take responsibility on his team for some of his clients and for business development. Antony and Amelia would provide Doug with an additional four years of compensation, and then he would take over their combined practice—a win-win for Amelia and Antony.

Expanding the Team's Offerings

In some cases, a team makes a hiring decision based on the need to expand their offerings. As our industry has progressed from trans-actional brokers to holistic planning, the need to add expertise to any team has increased. This becomes even more important as the affluence of your client base increases.

If a team is going to offer comprehensive planning and they don't have the expertise for intergenerational planning, risk manage-ment, or liability management covered, they can either outsource that expertise or add a new FA team member who has that exper-tise. For instance, Brian had extensive trust and intergenerational planning experience, and was employed by Merrill Lynch as a trust specialist. In his current position, he was being used as a resource to all the FAs in his market. One day, Brian was approached by a very successful team that had a high net worth clientele and a par-ticular need for trust and intergenerational planning. The team offered Brian a position on their team as an FA who would provide his expertise to their clients. Over the years Brian has had a signif-icant and positive impact on the team's production. He eventually became an integral part of the team's succession plan and is now a senior partner. He has helped make the team one of the high-est-producing teams in our industry.

Business Development

Every highly functioning team needs a marketing division. In some cases, senior advisors are not motivated to grow their own business, don't have the time, or don't have the expertise or interest to effec-tively acquire new high net worth clients. They are often faced with the decision to either become more engaged in proactive business development, or to hire another team member to focus on the marketing necessary to acquire new high net worth clients.

Typically, senior partners search for a young advisor to take on this role, but in most instances this is a mistake. Very few new advisors have the confidence and poise to attract new million-dollar clients for a team, and an experienced team doesn't need more small clients. A more attractive option is to add a team member who is experienced and who enjoys "the hunt" and the satisfaction of bringing on new business, and who is less interested in developing and implementing a wealth management process for the clients she brings in. This can again be a win-win situation: The business-development FA gets to do what she enjoys most and can delegate everything else to the other team members, and the team is able to build a marketing division if one doesn't exist. Again, the team must be willing to be generous in the team production splits with an effective business-development FA; otherwise that FA would be better off financially working on her own.

John is a good example of a real win-win situation for a team. He was a sole practitioner and enjoyed business development, but lacked the service capacity and the organizational skills to reach his full potential. An experienced team that was not meeting its growth goals recruited him. His only job was to get the senior team members in front of million-dollar prospects. The team gave him a generous split of 25 percent that amounted to a million-dollar production level, significantly more than he was producing on his own. The team measured John not only on his results but also on his activity and the quality of his pipeline—which he shared once a month at the team meeting. Since hiring John the team has met or exceeded its growth goals every year.

Deciding Between a Salaried Employee or a Financial Advisor

When hiring a relationship manager to handle smaller accounts do you compensate her as an FA with a split of the business, or pay her as an employee? My guidance on this decision is that when in doubt, add her as a salaried employee. Equity ownership is the most expensive form of compensation. The most important question the team should be able to answer on deciding whether or not to bring in a new team member as an FA or employee is "Are they capable of acquiring new million-dollar clients for the team?" If they can, and do, then they should be brought on as an FA. If they can't, they should be an employee.

Here's an example: If the team is doing $3 million and pays the RM as a 10 percent equity partner, then the RM compensation would be approximately $100,000 (33 percent of $300,000 production). Five years later, if the team is doing $6 million, then the RM is making $200,000 (33 percent of $600,00 production). However, if the team paid him $100,000 as an employee (combination of base salary and bonus), even if the RM got a 5 percent annual raise, after five years he would be at $130,000—which would be very generous compensation for an RM, but much less than the $200,000 he would receive as an equity partner.

It is always possible to transition a salaried employee to an FA as part of succession planning, when they can bring on new million-dollar clients. However, it is much harder to change someone's status from FA to employee than from employee to FA.

Hiring a Relationship Manager

Assigning smaller clients to a relationship manager should always be considered. By assigning smaller clients (below the top fifty) to a relationship manager, an FA partner can focus on providing her best clients with a high level of contact and service. By focusing on the most loyal affluent clients, FAs are likely to generate more referrals, expand wallet share, attract assets held away, have very high retention, and have more time for business development activities.

The relationship manager implements the team's wealth management process. It is recommended that the relationship manager be brought in as an employee and paid in the range of $75,000 to $120,000. The ideal workload assigned to a relationship manager is 120 to 150 households, and while some can certainly handle more, the service begins to be compromised. Once a relationship manager has more than 150 assigned households the team should consider hiring another relationship manager.

One of the analogies I like to use when a team is considering a relationship manager is the airline model. An airline is very clear about the way they reward their best and most loyal customers and how they treat their smaller customers. The most loyal customers are rewarded by first class upgrades, boarding first, no charge for luggage, and complimentary club membership at the airports. A second tier of good customers get economy plus with more legroom and early boarding. The infrequent flyers get the smallest seats in the back of the plane, are last to board, and likely do not experience any perks. If you apply this model to our business, then the top fifty clients are the FA's premier clients and get first class treatment; the next tier of clients are assigned to the relationship manager and get economy plus treatment, and the smallest clients are either divested or get minimal service. All clients should receive a basic level of service, but the team's practice will not be impacted if their smaller clients choose to leave and either work with another FA or a lower-cost option.

Hiring a Brand New FA

As I mentioned earlier, serious consideration needs to be given to bringing in a new hire as an employee or an equity partner. However, there are instances when it does make sense to add a new FA with no experience to the team as a small equity partner, if that person is capable of acquiring new million-dollar households. Many teams make the mistake of hiring a new FA because they want the FA to prospect, especially if the existing FAs no longer want to do it. Every FA team member must be committed to business-development activities if they want the team to grow. The last thing an experienced FA team needs is more small clients; in fact, the opposite is true, as they likely need to divest small clients.

New FAs that can bring in new million-dollar-plus relationships shouldn't be assigned any other responsibilities. Teams often bring on new advisors and assign them responsibilities for smaller clients, planning, and administrative tasks, as well as business development. If you assign them non-business development responsibilities they will gravitate toward those responsibilities instead of business development. Business development is the most challenging of all activities that an FA does, because rejection is inevitable with prospecting.

There is a notable exception for bringing on a new FA whose primary responsibility is not business development, and that is when the new FA is being hired as part of a succession plan. In that case, the new advisor has a clear role to be groomed to take over a portion of the practice. In some cases, this is a child of one of the senior team members.

If the new FA hire demonstrates the ability to bring in new affluent clients she must be recognized and rewarded early in her career, or the team faces the risk of losing her to an increased equity split by another team. A good example of this is when a professional athlete is paid a base salary until he is able to prove himself. If he emerges as a star performer, when it's time to renew his contract the team must be willing to pay him a premium or they face the risk of losing him to another team.

Hiring an Administrative Employee

As mentioned earlier, an administrative employee should be hired if the FAs are engaging in non-big three activities and these tasks can't be delegated to existing administrative support. In the case of several of the highest-producing teams, they actually hired junior administrative assistants for their most experienced administrative assistants. The team felt like the most experienced administrative assistants needed to be dedicated to providing outstanding service to their best clients, and these assistants needed to delegate many of the operational tasks in order to focus their time and attention on the team's best clients.

HOW TO HIRE

In my experience of hiring over five hundred individuals as a Merrill Lynch manager, I have come to the conclusion that the single best indicator of future success is an individual's past success. I believe that winners are hardwired to win; if an individual has demonstrated a consistent pattern throughout her career of successes, then her successes are most likely to continue. A highly functioning team needs to have overachievers—individuals who achieve beyond expectations.

The criteria for hiring based on an individual's track record applies to every position on the team. No matter what the job description is or the role that needs to be filled, past success is the best measure for future performance and increases the probability that you will make a successful hiring decision. The more examples a candidate has of tangible achievements, the better.

It is also important that successes are quantifiable. Examples could include:

- Where did they rank among their peers doing the same job?
- What were their past ratings for performance?
- What are some examples of specific accomplishments?
- What are some examples of overachievement?

THE BEST INTERVIEW QUESTIONS

Whenever I interviewed candidates for jobs, I used a variety of questions that were meant to predict future success. Over the years, I determined the single best interview question is:

"I would like for you to share with me your story and every quantifiable accomplishment and achievement that you consider significant in your life. This is an open-book test and the more quantifiable achievements you've had, the more likely you will be hired."

The following are some of the interview questions and likely answers that many of the best practicing teams used:

- *What are you most proud of in your life?* A good answer would include specific achievements.
- *What are your biggest accomplishments?* A good answer would include a specific achievement or two in the workplace.
- *If you could design it, what would be a perfect job?* This question makes sure that the current job offer is consistent with the kind of job the candidate would like. It also gives the interviewer the chance to see what the applicant aspires to in the future.
- *What did you like and dislike about your past two or three jobs?* This question provides insight into the applicant's attitude; it is a way to see if this job is a good fit.
- *What is your vision for the ideal career path?* Again, the questions provide an opportunity for insight as to the applicant's future aspirations, how realistic they are, and if the team can fulfill those aspirations.

Sourcing New Team Members

Once the team determines what its hiring needs are, it should develop a written job description. Once the written job description is complete, the following are potential sources that the team should use for sourcing the new hire:

- **Promoting existing team members.** Is the person with the skills you're looking for already on the team in a lower position?

- **Family members.** A team member's adult children might be qualified and interested in joining the team. I know many FA partners that have brought on their adult children as new FAs as part of their succession plan.
- **Online sourcing.** There are many internet sites for job postings that can used at a lower cost than advertising in local newspapers. LinkedIn is another excellent resource.
- **Office sourcing.** Often the local branch office of a large financial services company receives resumes from potential candidates that can be reviewed.
- **Other employees.** Within a branch office there may be employees outside of the team that could be considered potential candidates.
- **Clients.** This is one of the best but most underutilized sources for new hires. The team's clients should be provided with the written job description and asked if they know individuals that might be qualified candidates for open positions.
- **College job placements.** Local colleges, graduate schools, and trade schools should be contacted with written job descriptions for which their graduates might be appropriate candidates.
- **Professionals.** CPAs and attorneys that are part of the team's professional referral network can be contacted about junior or mid-tier hires. CPAs and attorneys they might know could be excellent candidates for relationship manager or planning specialist roles.
- **Service providers.** Team members should always be on the lookout for potential candidates as they deal with other service providers in their life. I can remember hiring an outstanding FA that I sourced through a men's clothing sales associate who sold me suits at Nordstrom's.
- **Wholesalers.** This is another underutilized hiring source. Wholesalers have a broad reach and come in contact with

many individuals who could be potential hires from other financial services firms.

TRAINING NEW HIRES

Hiring a qualified candidate without proper training can derail his success. A good hire deserves to have good training, and when this occurs the probability of him being a successful hire is greatly increased. If a team has a thoughtful hiring process then they must commit to having a good training process. Investing time up front in training is the best investment a team can make in a new hire.

There are three components that provide the foundation for any effective training process:

- **Written development plan.** The written plan should include a specific training plan for the new hire. The responsibilities should be clear, as well as the expectations. It should include a weekly developmental meeting and opportunities to shadow and observe members of the team that she will be reporting to. A checklist of skills she needs to master in order to perform her job needs to be provided, as well as a timeline and guidance that shows who is responsible for ensuring those skills are mastered.

- **Weekly developmental meeting.** The new employee should have a weekly meeting with the person he is reporting to so the supervisor can review responsibilities, answer questions, provide guidance, and review performance. This weekly meeting can also be used to talk through challenges the new hire has faced since the last meeting. The team member responsible for his training should be on the lookout for good performance to recognize and performance that needs to be improved. It's also important to check in on the new hire's feelings about the job, and give him an opportunity for candid feedback on how he feels things are going, especially during the first ninety days. One of the best training methods is to share case studies during the weekly meetings that apply to the new hire's responsibilities.

- **Job shadowing.** A new hire can shadow the team member that she is reporting to. This gives the new hire the opportunity to observe the behaviors and tasks from an experienced team member that she will be responsible for doing. For example, a new relationship manager can observe a senior team member conduct a client review, and debrief with the senior FA after the review is completed.

HIRING CHECKLIST

- ❑ Has your team developed a hiring process for new members of your team?
- ❑ Has your team developed a training process for each job position to include a written development plan, a weekly developmental meeting, and job shadowing?
- ❑ Is there a need to add an experienced FA to your team?
- ❑ Have you decided if new team members will be salaried employees or FAs?
- ❑ Do you need a relationship manager?
- ❑ Do you need to add an FA with no experience?
- ❑ Are all the FA team members focused on big three activities and does the team have the capacity for them to delegate all other non-big three tasks?
- ❑ Does your team have a ninety-day probationary period to evaluate the performance and attitude of new hires?
- ❑ Has your team developed sources for new hires when needed for each position?
- ❑ Has your team done a thoughtful analysis of what roles it needs to grow the practice, and what types of new team members need to be brought in to fill those roles?

9

The Product

A WORLD-CLASS OFFERING

A highly functioning team provides great value to the team's clients. However, if that value isn't articulated clearly to the team's clientele, the team will never leverage its full potential. That is the fundamental reason that a highly functioning team must develop and deliver a world-class offering for prospective and existing clients—and just as importantly, be able to clearly articulate that offering.

The advisors I interviewed all stressed the importance of delivering a superior offering to their clients and developing a value proposition. Developing a strong offering and articulating that offering is more complicated for a team than a sole practitioner, if only in terms of getting everyone on the same page. Yet a team's offering can be much more powerful than one coming from a sole practitioner. A team will always have more resources, more combined experience, more expertise, and the opportunity to provide superior service.

A well-thought-out offering helps the team acquire new clients. If the team wants to receive referrals, their existing clients must understand the team's offering clearly and be able to share it. If a client says to a friend, "You should talk to my advisor because they do a good job for me," it isn't a very compelling reason to switch from one advisor to another. However, if the client is able to say to a friend who is retiring, "You should talk to my advisor and his team because they specialize in helping their clients meet their cash flow needs in retirement," that provides a reason for the potential referral to be open to an introduction.

At my company, Altius Learning, we have incorporated this team best practice. We hired a consultant who interviewed every member of our team about what value we offered our clients, and how we were different. The consulting firm then analyzed the input and determined that there were two primary categories that all of the comments fit into:

1. All of our team members had been financial advisors or managers of financial advisors. This extensive experience set us apart from our competitors. Specifically, it gave us credibility and the ability to relate and connect closely with our financial advisor clientele.

2. We provide prescriptive, tactical, reality-based training, rather than just the "why" it needs to get done. Our stength is focused on implementation of proven strategies.

The consultant then helped us weave these two competitive differences into a value proposition. Once we had developed a thoughtful value proposition we now include it in all of our marketing materials, our website, and our social media sites. More importantly, every one of our team members internalized our value proposition and can effectively communicate it with prospective and existing clients. We are always on the same page and it became part of our team's DNA.

DEVELOPING A WORLD-CLASS OFFERING

We believe there are five cornerstones required to provide a world-class offering:

1. Trust
2. Discovery process
3. Goal-based planning and investing

4. Investment strategy and process

5. Client reviews

These five cornerstones must be included and consistently delivered to your clients at a high level. If you are able to do that and then articulate your offering through your team's value proposition, you will have a significant competitive advantage.

My intent for the remainder of this chapter is to provide you with guidance for how to incorporate these essential cornerstones into your team practices. Your team's offering can include other elements beyond these five cornerstones, but they are the foundation from which a world-class offering is built.

TRUST

Trust is the foundation from which a superior team offering is based. Without trust between the client and the team nothing else matters. Trust is based on three essential components:

1. **Ethical Behavior.** This is the most basic level of trust. Clients both consciously and unconsciously evaluate whether their advisors do what they say they are going to do. If the advisor's actions and words consistently match up, this level of trust is achieved over time.

2. **Technical Competency.** This is the belief by clients that their advisory team is capable of guiding them to their financial goals. A good analogy is when you are in a plane, do you have confidence that the pilot can safely get you where you need to go.

3. **Personal Stake.** This level of trust is achieved when clients believe their advisor cares deeply about them and their family, and is committed to helping them achieve their financial goals.

Each of these trust components must be present for the advisor to reach the highest level of trust with their clients. The following actions are necessary for a team to develop a high level of trust with their clients:

- Overcommunicate, keeping clients informed and being responsive to client requests. The number one reason clients leave a team is lack of communication.
- Continually remind your client how your various processes fit into their experience, which was outlined at the onset of the relationship.
- Share any member of the team's professional development achievements as a reminder that the team is committed to ongoing accreditations during the annual client review.
- Continue to educate your clients on financial issues and solutions.
- Include other experts such as CPAs and attorneys as you quarterback the delivery and implementation of wealth-management solutions.
- Emphasize the team's expertise and experience.
- During annual reviews, have a team agenda item that high-lights how the team improved their competency.
- During the annual review have a team agenda item that asks how the team can improve their offering; ask what the client feels the team has done best.

A team also needs to avoid practices that will erode trust with clients:

- Constant change in the way your team does things.
- Undercommunicating and not responding to clients' requests in a timely fashion.

- Lack of pricing transparency and a failure to link price to value.
- Lack of preparation when conducting client reviews, responding to clients' requests, or resolving client problems.
- Failure to back up your words with actions.

Building trust with new clients is essential: Once trust is gained it defines the quality of the relationship. The following are trust-building activities that should be done as a team best practice for new clients.

- Introduce team members to new clients by role and functionality and include any accreditations or certifications that support their technical competency.
- Educate your new clients. Spend the extra time to help them understand the options available to them. Explain the pros and cons of what you believe are the optimal strategies to achieve their goals.
- Describe the client experience your team delivers as part of your onboarding process, including your service model commitment, your client communication, your relationship management process, and your client review process.
- Talk about your team's commitment to ongoing professional development and how that benefits clients.

Just like with existing clients, the team needs to avoid practices that will erode trust with new clients. Avoid the following:

- Overpromising or not managing expectations for the onboarding process. For example, forgetting to include all the necessary paperwork, or going back to the client on multiple occasions to create more paperwork.

- Early failure to deliver what you represented to be the client experience. For example, you skip over a deep discovery process and jump straight into "how to invest money."
- Poor listening skills; not including all parties of a client relationship in the discussion.
- Not delivering a consistent client experience.

DISCOVERY

Deep discovery defines the client relationship. The discovery process includes an early opportunity to build trust with a new client and determine if there is the right fit. If it is determined that there is not a good fit during the discovery process, the team is better off walking away from the opportunity and referring the prospective client to a team where the fit might be better.

Deep discovery helps to establish client goals, risk tolerance, planning and investment strategy, and the opportunity to outline the team's value proposition. Other benefits of a deep discovery process include the opportunity to introduce the rules of engagement, including what the client can expect from the team and what the team expects from its clients. Again, this will help determine if there is a good fit.

There are six steps that define a world-class discovery process:

1. Discovery meetings should be held in person and include both the decisionmaker and her significant other. Additionally, other members of the team should be present to reinforce the message that you are a team rather than a sole practitioner.

2. An optimal discovery meeting is between one and two hours. The length and complexity of the meeting is driven by the client's circumstances. The bulk of the meeting (80 percent) should be devoted to gaining a full understanding of the client's

circumstances. A small amount of time should be allotted toward an explanation of your wealth management value proposition. If the team does most of the speaking, to the point where the meeting feels more like a presentation to the client, you lose. If the client does most of the speaking, you win.

3. Engage in a complete discussion of four big questions:

   - Why do you have money and what does it mean to you?
   - What do you want your wealth to do for you?
   - What are your fears about money?
   - What worries you most about investments?

4. Learn everything you can about the client's investment history.

5. Discuss what constitutes "safe" assets versus "risky assets."

6. Examine and discuss volatility risk, portfolio fluctuation versus lifestyle risk, and cash flow shortfalls.

Discovery Meeting Interview Guide

1. Relationships

☞ Tell me about yourselves and your family.

☞ What is the typical longevity in your family?

☞ Which family member relationships (spouse, children, siblings, parents) are the most important ones to you?

☞ Do you have any special needs in your family?

☞ How important are the relationships with people you work with?

☞ How important are relationships with people in your community?

☞ What is your religious orientation? How important are your relationships with your religion?

☛ What schools did you go to? How important is your relationship with these schools?

2. GOALS

☛ What would you like to achieve with your money?

☛ When it comes to money and your finances, what concerns you?

☛ What do you do (or want to do) for your children?

☛ What do you do (or want to do) for your parents?

☛ What do you do (or want to do) for other family members or close friends?

☛ What are your quality-of-life desires (houses, boats, cars, second homes, etc.)?

☛ What are your professional goals?

☛ At what age would you like to retire and on what monthly income (after tax)?

☛ How will you create this income?

☛ What are you most looking forward to when you retire?

☛ Are there any short-term needs (in the next twelve to eighteen months) which need to be considered in your investment plan (home repairs or remodeling, travel, gifts, taxes due, etc.)?

☛ If you did not have to work anymore, what would you do?

3. ASSETS

☛ Do you have an estate attorney? How do you feel about that relationship?

☛ Do you have a CPA or tax advisor? How do you feel about that relationship?

☞ Do you have a life insurance agent? How do you feel about that relationship?

☞ Do you have a private banker? How do you feel about that relationship?

☞ What were your best and worst experiences with a professional advisor?

☞ Of late, how frequently have you switched professional advisors?

4. PROCESS

☞ Who or what are your chief information sources regarding financial decisions?

☞ How involved do you like to be in the management of your investments?

☞ Who else do you want involved in the management of your finances?

☞ Who manages the family finances?

☞ How many face-to-face meetings would you like over the course of a year?

☞ How often would you like phone updates on your accounts?

☞ Do you want to be contacted by email?

☞ What security measures do you want to see used to protect your personal and financial information?

☞ Do you use any financial software in managing your finances?

5. INTERESTS

☞ What are your major interests?

☞ Do you follow sports? Who are your favorite teams?

☞ What are your favorite types of television programs and movies?

☞ What do you read?

☞ Do you have any health concerns or issues?

☞ Do you have a workout or fitness program?

☞ What are your hobbies?

☞ Do you speak a second language?

☞ What would be an ideal weekend for you?

☞ What would be an ideal vacation for you?

☞ What charitable causes do you donate to?

☞ What charitable causes do you volunteer for?

6. VALUES

☞ What is important to you about money?

☞ Is there anything I should know about you that I did not ask you?

☞ Why do you have money?

☞ Is there anything else I should know?

GOAL-BASED PLANNING AND INVESTING

Affluent individuals are most interested in achieving their financial goals—period. Highly functioning teams make goal-based investing a cornerstone of their offering because that is really what their affluent clients want.

The simplest way to define goal-based investing is that it is the "sum total of all current and future liabilities." I believe Andrew Rudd, co-founder and former chairman and CEO of Barra, Inc., provides an excellent description of goal-based investing:

"The financial goals of an investor are the most important components of the wealth management process, and these goals are the reason people invest their money. Therefore, the funding of one's goals must be the primary focus of the wealth-management strategy."

Goal-based investing is the link between discovery and investment process. It focuses on achieving goals regardless of market behavior. This approach also builds clients' trust because the advisory team is focused on what's most important to the client. Teams that focus their offering on goal-based investing and include that focus in their value proposition will have a distinct competitive advantage over teams that don't.

There are two priorities in goal-based investing: determining cash flow goals and determining the outcome certainty of those goals. Advisory teams that focus on goal-based investing find that it's rarely limited to portfolio issues and thus place a higher priority on meeting client goals than on short-term portfolio returns.

In incorporating goal-based investing in your team's offering I would recommend following these five best practices:

1. Use the discovery interview guide to establish or reaffirm client goals. It is never too late to go deep with these questions. If you can't currently answer every question in the guide, commit to doing so in the near future.

2. Assist clients with defining their goals. Discuss their spending and saving habits and their impact on long-term goal attainment. Review minimum, desired, and aspirational goals with clients. Determine a client's ability to maintain his desired lifestyle after retirement, demonstrating how you can guide him to the required cash flow.

3. Evaluate the wealth management plan you have been operating with, focusing on whether it includes all of your client's goals. Assess if the plan provides for a minimum income level regardless of market performance.

4. Perform a complete asset review profile, focusing on assets held away. These away assets would include retirement plan assets, deferred compensation plans, and other investment accounts. These outside assets should be cataloged and referenced in ongoing client communication. The advisory team should make a strong case for why it is in the client's best interest to consolidate all their assets with the team.

5. Explain to your client that her real investment risk is not underperforming a benchmark, but failure to reach her goals. Get the team's clients to recalibrate success as progress against goals and desired outcomes given their risk tolerance. Have clients think about evaluating the team's performance based on the success of progress toward goal achievement rather than short-term market performance as defined by an arbitrary index.

INVESTMENT AND STRATEGY PROCESS

It is beyond the scope of this book to provide an in-depth discussion of portfolio management and investment strategy. However, the top advisors on highly functioning teams emphasize the team's investment process and the significance that process has on the achievement of their affluent clients' goals.

There are eight characteristics that top advisors employ in their investment process:

1. Possess a clearly defined, disciplined investment process and be able to explain it to any prospect.

2. Educate clients on the investment process so they clearly understand it—this is a must do in order to build client trust and advocacy.

3. Use asset allocation as both a risk-management and a performance-building tool.

4. Having a macro view of the economic landscape is a necessity. Be able to articulate that view to clients and prospects.

5. Maintain a high conviction investment strategy and use model portfolios to bring scale to the team's practice.

6. Don't chase investment fads, and take a stand against extremes.

7. Performance reporting is a critical tool in maintaining client communication.

8. Maintain a conservative bias toward investing. Affluent individuals would rather make less than lose more, so managing risk is among the highest priorities of the investment process.

If you are implementing these eight characteristics, they validate your current process, and if not, I would encourage you to incorporate them. These eight characteristics offer a macro view that I believe teams should incorporate in their offering. However, it's also important to establish the team's core belief on investing that is unique to its practice. There can be different ways in which a team invests its client's assets. These core beliefs afford a clear distinction in the way the advisory team can differentiate itself. The important consideration is that these investment core beliefs are shared among the team's members, are consistently followed, and can be clearly articulated.

The following core belief shows a thoughtful conviction by a team. In fact, the top advisor that heads this team believes so strongly in this investment process that it is a core component of the team's value proposition.

Team Core Belief Example

- Buy stocks and high-beta assets when most investors are showing high levels of pessimism and fear.
- Reduce exposure in stocks and high-beta assets when most investors are overly optimistic and overly confident.
- Over time, higher yield stocks outperform lower yielding stocks and with less risk.
- Common stocks of companies that raise their dividends perform considerably better than those that don't.
- Common stocks of companies that deliver better than expected earnings (earnings surprise) outperform those that don't.
- Low P/E stocks outperform high P/E stocks over a complete market cycle.

CLIENT REVIEWS

We have found that the highest-functioning teams are committed to a formal review process, because it brings the wealth management offering to life. As financial advisors, what you provide your client is intangible—you can't touch it, smell it, or feel it. The review process turns the intangible offering of money into a tangible offering. By reviewing a client's progress toward his goals, review of his plan, and a discussion of his ongoing financial needs and solutions, the team is making their wealth management process "real" and something that the client can see and react to.

The purpose of client review is to evaluate the client's portfolio performance and her progress towards her goals, including funding the liabilities those goals represent. It also gives the team the opportunity to update their client's profile, educate the client, and gather feedback. Finally, it gives the team the opportunity to review the financial plan and update and modify it as needed.

It is recommended that the following best practices be included in the annual review. It may not be appropriate to cover all of them during the shorter more informal quarterly reviews. The best practices highly functioning teams use in the review process include:

- Utilize a checklist or template to assist your team in the preparation of a review.
- Use an agenda for all meetings, regardless of frequency and location. A sample client review agenda is included below.
- Conduct annual, in-person reviews. Annual reviews generally last an hour. Quarterly or semiannuals are dictated by your segmented client service model as a guideline. For the best clients, the second quarter (or semiannual review) should be done in person and lasts from thirty to sixty minutes, and quarterly reviews are typically twenty to thirty minutes in length.
- Spread annual reviews over the course of the year using the client's anniversary or birthdate.
- As part of building strong client loyalty, reconnect personally with the clients.
- Review your client's goals and objectives and tie the discussion into your investment strategy and progress toward the client's goals. Use this as an opportunity to reiterate your core investment beliefs.
- Address any current wealth management planning needs and action steps. Include functional expertise from other team members, internal specialists at your firm, or external advisors such as CPAs or an attorney.
- Gather feedback on their perspective of the client experience and their perspective on the portfolio's performance. Review the value you are delivering and when appropriate, how it supports your pricing model.
- Summarize the discussion and review next steps at the conclusion of the review.

Sample Agenda Template

Note: this agenda can be expanded or contracted depending on whether the review is annual, semiannual, or quarterly.

- **Opening:** reconnect with the client, build rapport, reconfirm the purpose of the review session, and review the agenda so the client knows what is to be discussed during the review.

- **Client Update:** update the client profile, confirm the original goals, update the client balance sheet.

- **Performance Review:** review both portfolio performance and progress toward originally identified goals. Include firm-provided reporting metrics and cumulative progress reporting against a specific goal such as "building an increasing income for retirement."

- **Market Perspective:** this is an opportunity to communicate current outlook on the markets, economy, and how the portfolio strategy is constructed.

- **Wealth Management Planning:** review progress and implementation of other wealth management solutions, for example estate planning and applicable document work, funding of trusts, etc.

- **Value Discussion:** an opportunity during the review to build trust, identify ways that the team is providing value, discuss pricing and transparency, and gather feedback from the client about the client's wealth management experience, and service.

- **Assets Held Away:** positioning statement.

- **Offer to Help:** opportunity to have a referral discussion.

VALUE PROPOSITION

A strong value proposition enables the team's client to advocate for the team through referrals and provides a compelling case for prospects to transfer their assets to the team and reinforces for existing clients the value the team provides them.

At Altius Learning when we guide teams toward developing a value proposition to reflect their offering we ask them to consider the following:

- **Who is your target client?** Any team wants the target client to be able to relate and identify with the value proposition and feel like it was customized to her unique and specific needs.

- **What are you most proud of—what are the signatures of the team's practice?** We want teams to focus on the three or four signatures of their practice and build them into their value proposition. Examples could include the cumulative years of experience of the team, professional designations team members might have, their wealth management process (holistic, goal-based planning, investment process), their service commitment, their specialization, client communication, or service commitment.

- **Do you have a specialized level of expertise and experience—a specific niche market?** Affluent individuals believe they are unique and there is a high appeal toward financial advisory teams that they believe have expertise and experience in their unique and complex financial issues. The team should include their specialization and expertise in their value proposition when approaching individuals that are in their niche.

- **How does your offering benefit your clients—what value do they receive by working with you?** It's not enough to say that the team has fifty years' experience; the value proposition should translate that fact into a client benefit by adding, "and with those years of experience we have developed the insight and perspective needed to guide our clients through all types of market conditions that only five decades of experience can bring."

- **How does your offering make you different?** The team value proposition needs to reflect how the team is different from other advisors.

VALUE PROPOSITION EXAMPLES

The value proposition can be expanded or condensed depending on the circumstances. If you have a scheduled prospect meeting than there is time to expand the value proposition. On the other hand, if you need to share the value proposition on the spot it would need to be condensed. The most important thing is that every member of your team is prepared to answer the all-important question, *"Why should I invest my money with your team?"* The response should be practiced, memorized, and expressed with the confidence and passion that only comes from preparation.

It is also important to note that the team's clients are well aware of their offering through hearing the value proposition. Not only does this reinforce the value they are receiving from the team, but it helps clients advocate working with your team to other people they know.

Value Proposition #1—Target Similar Cultural Heritage

You should consider working with our team because we bring a different perspective in working with clients than most financial advisors. As a first-generation immigrant, I understand personally the rewards of hard work and the need to both protect and grow your investments. I have dedicated my career to understanding the intricacies of financial planning, and with the resources available to me at (XYZ Financial) have developed a financial planning process that guides my select group of clients in reaching their financial goals. I am dedicated to my clientele and take the extra effort to stay abreast of the markets and how they affect the companies that my clients own and work for. If you entrust me with your assets you will be rewarded by my hard work, empathy, and world-class financial planning process.

Value Proposition #2—Senior Financial Advisor

You should consider working with me because I have accumulated over twenty-five years of experience. With that experience I have developed the insight and perspective to guide our clients through all types of market conditions that only two decades of experience can bring. Further, I have developed a thoughtful, disciplined investment process that has withstood the test of time, helping our clients successfully navigate through some of the most powerful bull markets and challenging bear markets. The cornerstone to our investment process is managing risk, with a priority of protecting wealth during the most challenging markets, ensuring that we don't put our clients' assets at undue risk.

My highest priority is to provide our clients with a service experience that exceeds their expectations by frequent contact, 24/7 availability, and proactive problem-solving to maximize their positive experience with our team and minimize the inconveniences.

Biotech and Pharma Executive Option

We have a division within our practice that for the past twenty years has specialized in working with senior biotech and pharma executives. This experience and expertise has enabled our team to be uniquely positioned to have an understanding of their unique needs and challenges, which include equity compensation, risk management, deferred compensation, and tax control.

BRANDING

The final step in the value proposition process is the branding of the team's offering. Every financial advisory team should focus on making sure that their target prospects know about their offering. The following are some examples of how the team can brand their offering:

- Team's website
- Marketing material
- Onboarding
- Social media profile
- Existing clients
- Professional referral network
- Prospects

10

Building a Marketing Division

I n my experience working with teams, I have found that most of them have a good product division (their wealth management offering) and a good service division, and a nonexistent marketing division. Yet without a marketing division a financial advisory team will never reach its full potential. The purpose of this chapter is to guide the team to build a highly effective marketing division.

TOP ADVISOR MINDSET

The teams with the highest functioning marketing divisions have incorporated the top advisor mindset into their practices. There are five distinct characteristics of the top advisor mindset that when applied to a team practice represent the foundation from which the marketing division is built. They include confidence, value proposition, optimism and opportunity, being uncomfortable, and time commitment. Maintaining a top advisor mindset represents the difference between knowing what to do and actually doing it.

Confidence

The essence of the confidence characteristic is the deep-seated belief that the team makes a positive and significant difference in the lives of their clients. This confidence is a core value of the team and every team member embraces it and incorporates it into every interaction with their clients. Confidence is built when the team can promote a world-class offering that guides their clients to reach their financial goals, their outstanding service model, and their accumulated years of experience that provide wisdom and perspective guiding clients though all types of market conditions. The team can then focus with confidence on their ability to handle every aspect of the client's financial life because they have deep relationships with their clients—they are a shareholder in clients' lives and always put their clients' interests first.

One of the most successful financial advisors in our industry defines this confidence level as having a "Financial Missionary Mindset" that guides him and his team in their acquisition efforts. He describes his team's missionary mindset in the following way:

"Missionaries go to underdeveloped countries and attempt to convert people in those countries to accept their religion. You can imagine how much rejection each missionary must experience. However, if you ask a missionary how they handle that rejection they will tell you that they don't feel badly for themselves but rather they feel badly for the people they weren't able to convert to their religion. They don't feel rejection—they feel sorry for those that they can't convince to believe.

Our team has adopted the financial missionary mindset and it is one of our core values. When we approach a prospective client, we believe we can and will make a positive difference in their life and they are fortunate to have the opportunity to work with us. If they don't accept our offer to help, then we don't feel rejected or bad about the lost opportunity—we feel sorry for them and move on to another prospective client that embraces our ability to help them."

We believe that when a financial advisory team adopts the financial missionary mindset, it takes the pain out of the inevitable rejections and defines the team marketing division philosophy.

Value Proposition

Based on my experience, individuals who have more than one million dollars to invest don't believe that there is much difference between financial advisory teams. A strong marketing division must be able to share how your team is different in the acquisition process. The value your team provides is by far the most compelling case to make.

The foundation from which the value proposition is built is the development by the team of a world-class offering, which we reviewed in Chapter 9. Taking that world-class offering and translating that into a value proposition incorporates five elements:

1. Who are you—what would your best clients say your strengths are?
2. Who is your competition? Who do you fear the most in a competitive situation? What are your competitive advantages?
3. Who are your ideal clients—will your value proposition resonate with them?
4. Build a story around your strengths. Focus on the three or four signatures of your practice—what you provide your clients that you are most proud of.
5. Consistently deliver on your value proposition.

Optimism and Opportunity

A core team value of successful and highly functioning teams is optimism. Their team leaders insist that all members have a positive and optimistic attitude. These teams recognize that there is never a lack of acquisition opportunity. As financial missionaries they are compelled and driven to put themselves in front of it through their activities. This provides a positive energy that is obvious and appreciated by the team's clientele.

Reviewing the following demographic data might be helpful for becoming more optimistic:

- In the United States today, there are approximately fifteen million individuals that have $1 million or more investable assets.

- According to a study of millionaires highlighted in the book *Cultivating the Middle-Class Millionaire,* approximately 15 percent make a significant financial advisor change each year.

- If 15 percent of millionaires are likely to make a significant advisor change in the next twelve months, that translates into 2.25 million individuals who have at least a million in investable assets. Those investors alone provide an enormous opportunity for financial advisory teams that have a strong marketing department and provides significant opportunities in most all markets in the U.S.

- The Baby Boomer generation needs retirement income planning with 10,000 retiring every day. There has never been a better time to be in this business for acquisition. A strong marketing division must be able to provide a compelling case why these affluent prospects should work with your team.

- Intergenerational transfer of wealth between the baby boomers and their parents is another significant opportunity and calls for financial advice and guidance.

It's never the case that opportunity doesn't exist to acquire new affluent clients—it's whether your team acts on that opportunity. For example, the Denver, Colorado metropolitan area (where I live and work) has approximately 60,000 households with a million dollars or more of investable assets. If 15 percent of those million-dollar households make a significant financial advisor change, then 10,000 local millionaires are in play every year. If a financial advisory team has a strong marketing division, acquiring 10 of those 10,000 millionaires in play is a no brainer.

Being Uncomfortable

A core value of the highest-functioning teams is that they are never complacent and are always uncomfortable: They want more. Having a strong marketing department requires commitment, discipline, process, and dedication. Establishing a strong marketing division is not easy, and it will only happen if the team is uncomfortable, wants to be better and is willing to accept the challenges of growth.

Time Commitment

The highest-functioning teams recognize that the right activities lead to the right results, and time must be spent consistently on those proven strategies that will bring in new affluent clients and assets. In fact, these teams recognize that the single most important factor in the success of their team's marketing division is how much time the FA team members spend on implementing these acquisition strategies.

When I ask teams what their biggest challenge is in their practices, often they tell me the acquisition of new affluent clients. I respond to this answer by asking them how much time did their team spend on activities that would bring in new affluent clients just one day before? Most of the time the response is "none." My response to that is, "Hope is not a viable acquisition strategy."

It's not any easier for high performers to do difficult tasks—the difference is they can make themselves do them. Their desire to grow and help prospective clients is greater than the discomfort required to achieve that growth.

In interviewing some of the most successful teams in our industry, I asked the FA team members how much time they spent every day implementing their team's chosen marketing strategies. On average, each team member spent at least 25 percent of their time engaging in proactive marketing—some combination of the seven core acquisition strategies.

Highly functioning teams need their FA team members to commit to a minimum of one hour a day implementing some combination of their chosen acquisition strategies. Once they have consistently achieved five hours a week of acquisition time, increase their time commitment to two hours a day or ten hours a week, which is the 25 percent time commitment that the best teams spend.

In the reminder of this chapter I will share with you the seven proven acquisition strategies that should be employed by your team's marketing division.

CLIENT REFERRALS

Having a consistent proactive client referral strategy must be an essential part of the team's marketing division. A consistent, proactive referral strategy produces the best acquisition results with a minimal amount of time invested—a winning combination.

Less than 10 percent of the thousands of advisors we work with every year have a consistent, proactive referral process. Yet according to Julia Littlechild, founder and CEO of Advisor Impact Research, 88 percent of highly satisfied clients feel comfortable providing a referral. This means that most teams are not taking advantage of what their clients are willing to provide.

All highly functioning teams should commit to a referral process that will close the gap between what loyal clients are willing to provide and how many quality referrals the team is receiving. The process starts with understanding why affluent investors provide referrals to their advisor. According to Julia Littlechild, there are four primary reasons why affluent investors refer:

1. *Reciprocity.* They like their advisory team and want to do something nice for them.
2. *Identification.* They identify someone in their social circle that has a specific need, such as a life transition, retirement, divorce, or a job change, and they believe their advisor can help that person.
3. *Financial planning.* Clients who do a financial plan with their advisors are more likely to provide referrals because of the deeper relationship that is developed through the planning process.
4. *Because the advisor reminded them.* The occasional professional ask can make a huge difference.

Identifying Loyal Clients

So much attention in our industry has been spent on finessing the right script and techniques, but not enough attention is spent on the importance of having a loyal client base. If a client is a loyal and raving fan, then having a perfect script is not very important. Your team's loyal clients are already willing to help, you just have to help them help you. On the other hand, if the client is either not satisfied or is just marginally satisfied with you, then the best script and techniques in the world won't generate referrals. In my experience if a client is loyal, your team just needs to incorporate a process that makes it easy to turn that loyalty into referrals.

My recommendation is to rate your clients on a 1 to 4 scale, and then focus your referral process only on those affluent clients who are either a 3 or a 4. Don't waste your time on the 1 and 2 rated clients:

- 4—most loyal
- 3—highly satisfied
- 2—satisfied
- 1—not satisfied

Most teams do not have a consistent proactive referral process in place. When asked why, the most common reasons I have heard are the following:

- *I don't want to put pressure on my clients.*
- *Referrals are about me, not my clients.*
- *I feel like a salesperson, not a professional advisor.*
- *My doctor doesn't ask me for referrals.*
- *I don't have a process I'm comfortable with.*
- *I don't want to appear needy or desperate for new clients.*

This way of thinking has to change. If you believe that any other advisor would not do a better job for your clients than you do, why wouldn't you want to make a positive difference for people your clients know? This is the financial missionary mindset.

You are offering your clients a gift, which is your ability to have a positive impact on the lives of their friends, colleagues, and family members. You have to assume you would do a better job for your client's colleagues, friends, and family members than the advisor those people currently use—again the missionary mindset. The benefit to the clients is they look like heroes for introducing friends to a world-class financial advisory team like yours.

Building a Consistent Referral Process

FA members should commit to having a meaningful referral discussion once a year with each of their loyal, affluent clients who are highly satisfied. This frequency can be increased, but once a year is enough to get a steady stream of quality referrals, while not so much that it takes away from the professionalism of the process. It is preferable for the advisors to have one "Academy Award winning" discussion than more frequent superficial and ineffective referral asks.

An annual discussion:

- Is done in person
- Is done at the end of a review
- Is well thought out and memorized
- Can include a specific name of someone you know they know who you would like to work with
- Makes it a brainstorming session rather than a "yes" or "no— I can't think of anyone"
- Provides the client with examples of people she knows going through "life transitions"
- Positions future events as way of introducing you to people he "thinks you should know"
- Asks the client to give the referral a heads up through a call or email that you will be contacting her

As an accountability tool, I strongly recommend that you develop a spreadsheet of your loyal and highly satisfied clients and put a check mark next to their name once you have had the annual referral conversation. The objective is to have a check next to each of these clients' names by the end of the year—whether they have provided a referral or not.

One way of helping your clients help you is to provide a name of someone you would like to meet that they know. The best source of names for you to provide to your clients can be found on the website of where they work. Keep track of who your clients know, what boards they sit on, who are their neighbors, what country clubs they belong to, etc.

LinkedIn is another excellent resource to help your clients help you. Connect with every loyal client you have on LinkedIn. You will then have access to their connections. The numbers and the process are powerful: 200 primary contacts will provide up to 40,000 potential connections. The information can be robust: It often includes work history, college attended, and outside interests. A best practice is to focus on people in same company.

Another way of helping your clients help you is by sharing the philosophy that people going through life transitions are the ones who need your help the most. Give them examples of life transitions—retiring or recently retired, loss of spouse to divorce or death, loss of parents and subsequent inheritance, selling their business or changing jobs. Letting your loyal clients know about your specialization and asking if they know anyone who could benefit from that specialization is also effective.

Often, even the most loyal clients can't describe or explain the value their advisors provide or how they are different. Make sure your value proposition is mentioned during the referral conversation so that clients understand how you are different. Then they can share your story with potential referrals. Tell the clients that all you need for them to mention is that they have had a favorable experience with you (mention your specialization), and ask referrals if they would be open to a short introductory conversation with you, and you will take care of the rest.

Team Accountability

During the team's marketing meeting all FA partners should share how many meaningful referral conversations they have had in the past month, and the result of those conversations. Challenges should be brought up and success stories highlighted.

STRATEGY #2
BUILDING A PROFESSIONAL REFERRAL NETWORK

One of the primary ways millionaires get their financial advisors is through a referral from another one of their trusted advisors—primarily their CPA or attorney. Building your own referral network is a strategy that should be incorporated into a team's marketing division. There is a five-step process for building this network. If this recommended process is followed, within twelve to eighteen months, the team will have three to five CPAs or attorneys who can provide one or two qualified referrals a year, resulting in at least five new high net worth clients annually.

STEP 1: Permission to Call Clients' CPA and Attorney

The first step is to contact each of the team's core affluent clients and ask permission to contact their CPA and attorney, with the goal of building a professional relationship with them for the benefit of the client. A master list should be developed with the names and contact information.

STEP 2: Contact the Professional Referral Source

Once permission has been granted and contact information received, FAs should contact their clients' CPAs and attorneys and suggest a meeting (perhaps a lunch meeting). In almost all cases the CPA or attorney will agree to this meeting because they understand it's in their best interest to have a relationship with their client's key advisors. It should be made clear that neither the financial advisor nor the potential professional referral source bills the client for this meeting.

STEP 3: First Meeting with the Professional Referral Source

The objective of this first meeting is to build a foundation for a good professional relationship. This means encouraging the professional referral source to talk about their practice in a friendly atmosphere. Examples of some of the questions you could ask might include

- How do you source new clients?
- What is your area of expertise?
- How long have you been a CPA?
- How is your practice organized?
- What are the challenges your practice faces?
- Have you built a strong relationship with another financial advisor?
- Why do your clients work with you?
- What is your ideal client?
- How do you get updated information about tax strategies related to your clients' investments?
- Are you licensed to provide investment advice?

At the end of the meeting, the FA should offer an invitation for a subsequent meeting to share with the potential referral source how specifically they work with the mutual client. In most cases if the advisor has done a good job of focusing on the potential referral source's practice the referral source will be open to learning more about the financial advisor.

STEP 4: Presentation Meeting with the Professional Referral Source

The purpose of the presentation meeting is to dispel the myth that most CPAs and attorneys have that financial advisors are commission-based salespeople that sell their firm's products. The presentation meeting should be organized in four parts:

1. Brief description of the financial advisor's team
2. Your value proposition
3. Brief description of the team's wealth management process
4. Brief demonstration of the tools the team uses to help clients reach their goals

The presentation meeting should be well-prepared and short—with an ideal time of thirty minutes. At the end of the presentation meeting the financial advisor should suggest that they maintain their professional relationship and offer to provide timely information that would be interesting and helpful to the CPA or attorney as it relates to taxes and investments. The potential referral source will always agree, which leads to the most important step in the process—the follow up.

STEP 5: The Follow-up

The good news in this process is that if you follow the first four steps then 80 percent of the team's core affluent CPAs and attorneys will agree to an offer to periodically stay in touch. The bad news is that if you don't do the follow-up step the process will not work. As you can imagine there is no shortage of financial advisory teams trying to get CPAs and attorneys to refer to them. However, very, very few are willing to make the necessary time commitment to turn these professionals into referral sources.

The reason the follow-up step is required is that CPAs and attorneys have too much to lose by referring their best clients to a financial advisor unless a strong relationship of trust is built. The mistake that most advisors make is that they don't invest enough time into building a relationship of trust, which can't be done without a real commitment to the process.

I recommend a monthly touch (either voice or face) driven by sending a piece of timely information that is relevant to the CPA's or attorney's practice and following up with a call to cover the piece in more detail. If the team is willing to invest some time to develop a "white paper library," that becomes the source of the monthly touch points. Some of these monthly touch points can include case studies of other clients in life transitions that the team helps and the sharing of the team's niche market expertise. This opens the door to discuss these options with the CPA and attorney to help their other clients who might be in similar life transitions or would benefit from the team's niche market expertise. At least four times a year, the monthly touch should be done in person. These personal meetings help further develop the required trusting relationship.

Team Accountability

This is a process that requires the entire team to be organized. The follow-up process can be delegated to a business development partner (if one exists) or a junior partner. The team can collaborate on building a high-quality white paper library. During team marketing meetings, each team member should report on the potential referral sources they are responsible for and get input from other team members on success stories, case studies, and ideas they are having in deepening relationships and generating referrals. Accountability and brainstorming are powerful forces that can help the team's success in developing a strong professional referral network.

EVENT MARKETING

Event marketing is an acquisition strategy that most of the top teams incorporate through their marketing division. This strategy is conducive to teams as multiple team members can work to fill the events with the right people. The teams that are most successful with event marketing incorporate five core principles that ensure acquisition success.

PRINCIPLE 1: Smaller Intimate Events (10 x 10 Rule)

The objectives of event marketing are for financial advisors to meet new prospective clients, to deepen relationships with existing prospects and professional referral sources, and to transition personal relationships into prospects. An added benefit is building stronger client relationships. These objectives can best be accomplished when the total number of attendees is between eight and twelve, with the ideal number being ten. If there are more than twelve participants the opportunities to interact and build relationships are limited.

However, because the ideal number of participants is ten it is necessary to have multiple events to get the numbers required to make this a successful acquisition strategy. In coaching advisory teams, I recommend the "10 x 10" approach—that is, ten events annually with ten participants at each event. This incorporates the intimate size with the scale necessary to generate at least five new high net worth clients annually.

One of the benefits of a team in utilizing this strategy is that each team member can be responsible for a number of the ten events—spreading the responsibility so that no one team member is overwhelmed with having to set up and fill ten events. For instance, if a team has two FA partners, each partner would be responsible for organizing and hosting five events a year. The partners could help each other fill the events by inviting each other's prospects and professional referral sources to each other's events.

PRINCIPLE 2: 50 percent non-clients

At least half the participants at each event should be non-clients. While it's important to have clients participate in the events, if the majority of participants are clients than it becomes a client appreciation event, not an acquisition strategy. However, there is real value in having some clients at each event, because it enables the FA to build stronger relationships with loyal clients, who can also be advocates of the team for the non-clients who are there.

There are four sources FAs should use to include at least 50 percent non-clients at each event:

- **Clients' guests.** Encourage clients to invite a guest that they enjoy spending time with that they think your team should know (this ensures qualified guests). In my experience, it takes four client invitations to produce one guest—however the percentage is typically higher when it's a couples event, yielding closer to a 50 percent success rate. A recommended strategy is during the annual referral conversation to mention that you would like to invite them to events and to think about guests that would be good introductions to the advisor. Another technique is to provide the client with a specific name of someone the FA would like her to invite. The source of these names could be someone the client has referenced in past conversations, someone she works with, or a neighbor. It also makes sense to ask for the guest's name in advance so the FA can send him an invitation and introduce herself to the guest in advance. Expected results—one non-client per event. Typically, one in three clients will bring a guest if asked, which makes it likely that there will be one or two qualified prospects as a result of asking clients to bring a guest.

- **Professional referral source.** This is an ideal way to enhance and develop deeper relationships with potential professional referral sources. Use the list of existing clients' CPAs and attorneys as referenced in the professional referral strategy. Encourage the professional referral sources to invite one of their good clients that the professional referral source enjoys spending time with that they think the advisor should know. Expected result—one non-client guest.

- **Right place—right people.** These are individuals that a FA knows personally who the FA would like as clients but has never talked with about working together professionally. By having them attend an event, these personal relationships can turn into potential clients. For the potential clients, seeing the advisor in a professional setting may help set the transition process in motion. Also, the event follow-up conversation will help transition an affluent acquaintance into a prospect. Expected result—one non-client guest.

- **Prospect pipeline.** These are individuals who are in the team prospect pipeline. A prospect is an affluent individual that the FA team has approached about working together who hasn't become a client yet. The value of inviting a prospect to the event is the opportunity to deepen the relationship, have the prospects interact with the team's clients, and have them see the advisor in a professional setting. Expected result—one non-client guest.

PRINCIPLE 3: "We Care" Rather Than "We Know"

Wealthy individuals are much more inclined to participate in a "We Care" fun event rather than a "We Know" educational event. One of the best ways to decide on fun client venues is to know what the team's clients like to do, and to organize events around the majority of the clients' interests. Most of the affluent clients' friends are people that like to do what the clients like to do.

However, it is essential that during the fun event the FA team member "says something smart" so that the FA team member can show off professionally. This allows non-clients to see the FA team member in his role as an FA even though the event venue is fun. The idea is to be brief but make a good professional impression. Examples of "smart" topics include investor psychology, market updates, the importance of goal-based investing, the power of asset allocation, five essential investor principles, or information tying the event venue to an investment-related topic.

The ideal time for this is ten minutes at the beginning of the event, which can be introduced in the following way, "*Before we start our event today I would be remiss if I didn't take a few minutes to share with you a few insights that you might find helpful as investors. . . .*"

PRINCIPLE 4: Plan Events Twelve Months in Advance

Schedule the team's ten events a year in advance. This gives the team a full year to fill the events with the right people—especially non-clients. There is upfront work to determine the dates, venues, and logistics, but once that work is done all that remains is filling the hundred spots. This schedule also provides the team with deadlines and the accountability to ensure the events are well-attended. Additionally, by scheduling the events six to twelve months in advance, you can fill events with "carry overs"—clients and guests who have had a scheduling conflict or canceled at the last minute.

PRINCIPLE 5: The Forty-eight Hour Follow-up Rule

It is *essential* that within forty-eight hours of an event every non-client be followed up with by an FA team member. At the event, the participants should be asked to sign in with their name, email address, and phone number. The importance of following up within forty-eight hours is after that the goodwill created by the event begins to disintegrate. The team needs to capitalize on the goodwill created, increasing the probability that an FA will get a meeting with the affluent prospects who attended.

Within forty-eight hours the following script should be used for all non-clients:

> *Mr./Ms. Prospect thank you for attending our event, I hope you had as good of a time as we had. I wanted to extend an invitation to you that I hope you accept. We believe our team is different from other financial advisors and we provide great value to our clients in guiding them in reaching their financial goals. I would like to invite you to an informal discovery meeting with the intent of getting to know each other better to see if we could potentially add value to your current financial situation.*
>
> *Will you accept my invitation?*

Team Accountability

During the team's annual strategic meeting the commitment to ten events should be made, the venues and dates determined, and FA team members should be assigned to run specific events. During the marketing team meetings, a progress report should be made by each team member on the status of their assigned events, and a solicitation for help can be addressed if needed.

STRATEGY #4

RIGHT PLACE—RIGHT PEOPLE

This strategy is based on team members putting themselves in position to be in the right place to meet the right people, with a transition plan in place to turn the "right people" into prospects. The right places can include nonprofit boards, country clubs, religious organizations, school boards, service organizations, neighborhood associations, and alumni boards.

Each FA team member should be able to develop a list of at least twenty-five individuals that they have personal relationships with who could become potential clients. Once that list has been developed a specific transition strategy should be assigned to each of those individuals. I would recommend choosing one of the following three strategies:

The Direct Approach

This approach should be used when the personal relationship is strongest and requires the missionary mindset—the strong conviction that the FA can make a positive difference in the life of her friend. This approach requires that the FA approach the personal contact and directly suggest they meet so that the advisor can share how she could add value to the contact's financial life. Please see the following script as an example of the direct approach:

Mr./Mrs. Personal Contact we have known each other for some time and I know you are an investor and you know I am a financial advisor. Our wealth management process is different from many other Financial Advisors and I feel good about the value we provide our clients. I wanted to ask you if you would be open to meet and let me share how I have helped my clients and see if I could add value to your current investment situation.

The Triggering Approach

This approach is best used with an individual that the FA has a personal relationship with who he sees on a regular basis but is not comfortable with using the direct approach. As the FA team member interacts with the personal relationship, he can ask deliberate questions that can trigger an offer to help the friend. The triggering opportunities are based on life transitions that the friends are going through. Examples of triggering questions could include:

- *"What's going in your life these days?"*
- *"What's new and different in your life?"*
- *"How is your business going?"*

- *"What challenges are you facing in your business these days?"*
- *"How long do you plan to continue to work?"* (Depending on age)

If the triggering questions provide a transition opportunity, I recommend that an FA wait a week and provide an offer to help by providing their professional expertise in that particular life transition to their friend through a meeting. This is no different than a doctor offering a friend assistance if they observed a symptom that required attention.

There will be cases when the questions do not produce a triggering response. However, if the FA is patient, deliberate, and continues to ask these questions there will eventually be a triggering opportunity.

MORE TRIGGER QUESTIONS

The Initial Ask

(choose one of the following):

- ➤ Mr./Ms. Prospect: What's going on in your life these days? (Divorce, inheritance, business sale, retirement, job change)
- ➤ Mr./Ms. Prospect: How much longer do you plan on working? (Retirement opportunity)
- ➤ Mr./Ms. Prospect: How is business going these days? What challenges do you have in your business? (Business sale, lending strategies, retirement plan, succession planning)

Follow-Up

(1–2 weeks later):

- ➤ Mr./Ms. Prospect I was thinking about the conversation we had a couple of weeks ago when you shared with ↓

me (1, 2, or 3 above). It occurred to me that many of my clients are in the same circumstances as you and face similar challenges. In thinking about your situation, I thought it might be helpful if we had an informal meeting where I could share with you some of the strategies I use with my clients to help them address the same issues that you described. Could I buy you a cup of coffee to discuss?

Event Invitation Approach

This approach should be used with personal relationships when the FA might not see a personal relationship frequently enough to use the triggering approach and feels the direct approach is not appropriate. The FA can invite this type of individual to one of the team's events. This strategy works for three reasons:

1. The personal relationship meets the team's other clients who often can be advocates.
2. The personal relationship gets to see the FA in action when the FA "says something smart."
3. It serves as a transition to the direct approach when the FA follows up forty-eight hours later.

Team members can use the following event invitation script:

I am hosting a cooking class/ golf outing/ fine dining event for my best clients and good friends and I wanted to extend you an invitation to join us (provide date and logistics). I would enjoy having you participate and I know you would enjoy the company of my other guests—would you be able to attend?

Team Accountability

During the marketing team meetings, each FA should review their right place/right people list and update the other team members on their progress and challenges of implementing these right place transition strategies.

ASSETS HELD AWAY

This is the single most powerful acquisition strategy that a financial advisory team can employ. The easiest assets that a team can acquire are those assets that their clients have away from them. This is truly the low hanging fruit, yet most advisory teams don't have a process for acquiring assets held away. There is a four-part strategy that will produce impressive acquisition results when the team incorporates it into their marketing division.

Discovery

Every FA team member must make a commitment to discover every client's assets held away. This can't be an estimate: It must be an accurate verification and updated every year. There are three primary ways to complete the discovery process:

1. *Financial plan.* By completing a financial plan the advisor will know where the client's assets held away are.
2. *Online financial balance sheet.* Most firms have an application that allows the client to provide online information about where all assets are held.
3. *Informal financial balance sheet.* The advisor positions the importance of knowledge of the client's complete financial picture so they have the context needed to provide the best possible financial advice.

Here's a script:

If I am doing my job correctly, my relationship with you should go beyond just advising you on the assets you have at our firm. As you know, asset allocation is a core part of our wealth management process, and I am comfortable that the assets that you have with me are properly allocated. However, I need to have an idea of how the assets you have with me relate to the asset allocation that you have at other places. It gives me the perspective and context that enables me to do the best possible job I can for you. I would also like to encourage you, as you feel comfortable, to consider consolidating all of your assets with me, so I can include everything in our wealth management process and simplify your financial life. Let's take a minute and allow me to build out your balance sheet.

Create a Client Prospect List

As the discovery process is being completed, each FA should transfer the information on assets held away onto a single spreadsheet by each client's name. This will become the best prospect list an FA will ever have—a client prospect list.

Assume Ownership

Once the FA knows where the affluent client's assets held away are, they need to assume ownership of those assets even if they aren't with them. By assuming ownership and referencing the away assets on a regular basis the FA is creating the perception that they are coordinating all of their client's assets. Examples of assuming ownership could include the following:

- Sharing asset allocation recommendations on all assets, including those held away
- Sending research reports and updates on equity positions on away assets

- Sharing investment ideas and encouraging the client to purchase with assets away and transferring
- Suggestions on relationship pricing and lower fees by moving all the assets
- Making the case that it's in the client's best interest to have one financial plan and one advisor to implement all aspects of the plan
- Providing market updates on all assets including those held away
- Making investment recommendations on assets held away

While I'm not a compliance expert with the pending DOL requirements for fiduciary responsibility on retirement assets, any recommendations or reference to assets away should be documented in the client's notes with the rationale behind those recommendations. Please consult your compliance manager to ensure compliance.

Positioning Statement

Each FA team member makes a positioning statement to each of their significant clients that makes the case that it's in the client's best interest to have all of their assets with the team. When I ask FAs if they think it's in the best interest of their clients to have all their assets with their team, they always say yes. Then, when I ask if their team is most qualified to be that team, they always say yes. My strong point is that if the advisor believes it's in the client's best interest they must strongly make the case. Clients pay advisors for their leadership and FAs owe their clients leadership. The following is my recommended positioning statement:

> Mr./Mrs. Client, it is my obligation to provide you with the best financial advice that I can give you. It's your choice if you want to follow my advice. In my professional opinion, it is in your best financial interest to consolidate all of your assets with one trusted financial advisor to guide

you toward the obtainment of your financial goals. It doesn't make sense to have multiple advisors providing you multiple opinions about investments and financial planning that could be conflicting. You are too busy to try to determine whose advice to follow under a variety of different situations and market conditions. I am capable and willing to be the advisor that coordinates every aspect of your financial life and would like you to consider me for that job.

Often the client will provide the objection "I don't want all my eggs in one basket." Here is the appropriate response to that objection:

I understand that you want to diversify your assets with different financial advisors, I have had clients in the past that felt the same way—however I want to say something as respectfully as I can, and that is you are making an emotional not a logical decision. The wealthiest individuals in America work with a family office that oversees and coordinates every aspect of their financial life and I would like to treat your assets the same way the wealthiest families do. Bill Gates delegates the management of all of his assets to one organization that oversees every aspect of his financial life.

The positioning statement should be brought up again every year until all available away assets are brought in. Each FA team member should state:

I know I have brought this subject up last year but I will continue to remind you of my intent to oversee all your assets because I believe it is in your best interests. You should always expect that I give you my best financial advice—would you reconsider transferring all of your assets to me?

Team Accountability

The team should have a master spreadsheet that shows the team's clients' away assets and where they are located. This spreadsheet should be reviewed and updated during the team's marketing meeting. This serves as an accountability tool and can provide recognition for each team member who acquires a portion of the away assets from their existing clients. It also provides a venue for each team member to brainstorm ideas for acquiring away assets, and for receiving input on challenges they might have in their acquisition efforts.

STRATEGY #6
PROSPECT PIPELINE

For a team's marketing division to be effective they must build and manage a prospect pipeline. The leading indicator of a team's acquisition success is the strength of their pipeline and how effectively they manage it. A prospect is defined as an affluent individual who the advisor has met with and offered to manage all or a portion of their investments, who meets the asset minimums the advisor is willing to work with, and who is receptive to the advisor staying in touch with her.

We have determined that for most teams, the ideal number of prospects is twenty-five per FA team member. As an example, fifty prospects should result in a 20 to 30 percent conversion of prospects to clients within twelve months. We have also found that twenty-five prospects per FA team member is a manageable number for a team. Once the pipeline is built to fifty prospects, whenever a new prospect is added, the weakest prospect is dropped. This results in a pipeline where the quality of potential clients continuously improves.

Treat Prospects Like Clients

Our strategy is for the advisor to treat his prospects as if they were already his best clients—building a case through his actions that the prospect is better off with him than with their current advisor. Our research shows that affluent clients prefer monthly contact from their advisors, including both face-to-face meetings and phone calls.

The advisor should always be thinking about ways she can develop better and deeper relationships with her prospect pipeline, and execute those strategies every month with every prospect. One of the most effective strategies is to email or send the prospect an idea, white paper, or recommendation and follow up with a call or face-to-face meeting. Other examples of potential prospect contact could include:

- Investment recommendations
- Asset allocation changes
- Research reports or opinion changes on a particular holding
- An invitation to an event
- A birthday call
- The acknowledgement of a significant event in their family's lives

We have found that if the team builds their pipeline to twenty-five prospects per FA team member and effectively manages their pipeline, they can expect to convert at least 25 percent of those prospects to affluent clients every year. The cornerstone of this process is for the advisor to position themselves as a strong second choice with their prospects. Typically, there is no competition for the second spot because when most advisors can't convert a prospect to a client right away, they either discard the lead or file the prospect away with good intentions to follow up, but never do. As a result of positioning themselves as a strong second, the advisor has no competition for that spot and when the current advisor makes a mistake and the client is looking for other options, the second advisor moves up to the primary position.

Team Accountability

During the team's marketing meeting the pipeline should be reviewed with each FA team member giving a brief update on assigned prospects. This gives each team member an opportunity to get input from other team members for ideas on staying relevant to their prospects, overcoming specific challenges, and discussing when to drop a prospect from the pipeline. It also is an accountability tool that keeps the FA team members cultivating their prospects and for recognizing them when a prospect is converted to a client.

STRATEGY #7
NICHE MARKETING

This strategy has a proven upside in developing new clients and has no downside—a winning combination. Niche marketing is effective because as individuals become more affluent they feel entitled to work with financial advisors who specialize in their occupation or stage of life and who understand their perceived unique and complex financial issues. Developing a specialization can also provide a compelling reason for a prospect to transfer his relationship to the team if he perceives that the team specializes in his profession or stage of life and his current advisor does not have that expertise.

Another benefit of niche marketing is that in most professions it's a small world, and if the team develops a strong reputation within a profession it becomes much easier to get references and generate referrals from individuals within that profession. These references and referrals are much more impactful when they come from within. If a team develops and has a specialization within a profession they will eliminate the majority of their competitors. The reason is that most teams have not taken the time or made the commitment to specialize.

Finally, and perhaps the most compelling reason that teams should develop a specialization is that the most successful acquirers are specialists. In my book, *The Million-Dollar Financial Advisor*, I interviewed many of the most successful advisors in the industry, and all of them considered themselves to be specialists.

The biggest objection that advisory teams have in developing a specialization and engaging in niche marketing is that it precludes them from attracting affluent individuals who are not in their area of specialization. There is a simple solution to this dilemma and that is for the team to position their niche market as a division within their practice. Having a division or divisions within a practice is a model that many larger law and tax accounting firms have; the same model can apply to financial advisory teams. By positioning the divisions within our practice the advisory team is getting the full benefit of niche marketing and not giving up the opportunity to work with affluent individuals who are not part of their niche marketing specialization.

The following responses serve as an example:

- *"In our team, we have a division that has developed an expertise in single women going through life transitions"*
- *"In our team, we have two divisions: one that specializes in corporate executives and the other with medical professionals"*

DEVELOPING A NICHE MARKET PLAN

I would recommend that the team develop a formal niche-marketing plan that is based on the following four concepts.

Identify the Niche

If the team does not have a niche/specialization they need to identify one. When I guide teams on how to identify a niche I ask them to consider the following options:

1. **Natural market.** Identify the occupations (retirement counts as an occupation) of the team's best clients to determine if the team has a natural market that could be the basis of the team's niche market.

2. **Past background.** Often FA team members might have had a career prior to becoming financial advisors. They may know affluent individuals in that profession and how to reach them. Additionally, they understand and can relate to that type of professional's unique and complex financial issues and challenges. It becomes a powerful connector if prospects within an occupation know an advisor understands their profession through personal experience.

3. **Market demographics.** In every city, there as at least one strong affluent demographic. Identify the natural affluent demographic in your market and capitalize on the demographic by developing a specialization within that occupation or stage of life. Examples include:

    Silicon Valley: software technology entrepreneurs
    Minneapolis: Fortune 1000 executives
    New York: financial services executives
    Atlanta: cable technology executives and business owners
    Denver: entrepreneurs

4. **Default niche.** Develop an expertise and provide it to individuals who are transitioning from the accumulation of wealth to the distribution of wealth—the Baby Boomer generation. This niche is large—80 million individuals with 10,000 of them retiring every day. These people are focused on how to generate the cash flow they need to live the way they want when they choose not to work anymore. An advisory team that can help them solve that need will be in very high demand for the foreseeable future. While many teams may have this expertise,

if they haven't developed and implemented a niche marketing plan they have not capitalized on the power of niche marketing.

Gain Expertise

The value to the affluent client in working with a team that specializes in their profession or stage of life is the expertise the team offers. As part of a team niche market plan the team must determine if they have the requisite expertise to effectively serve their niche market. If they don't, they need to develop a plan for developing that expertise. It's also a good practice to interview the team's clients who are in the niche on which the team is focused to get advice on how best to approach that niche. The good news for most teams is that their firms provide specialists and resources for almost any niche market.

Create a Marketing Plan

To leverage the team's specialization, they need to develop a marketing plan on how to incorporate existing acquisition strategies into their niche market plan. The following are ways that the team can leverage their niche marketing into the other six core acquisition strategies:

1. **Client Referrals.** Referrals are significantly increased if the team's niche is well-described during the annual review and referral conversation. Every client of the team should be aware of the team's niche markets so they can help identify new prospects that could benefit from the team's expertise. This is especially effective for clients who work within the occupation that team specializes in, following the "small world" concept mentioned early in this chapter: This is a classic example of helping your clients help you.

2. **Professional Referral Network.** There are two reasons that CPAs refer their clients to a financial advisor: "they like and trust"

the advisor and "they believe the advisor has a level of expertise that would benefit their clients." By sharing information with the professional referral network, these referring professionals can identify their clients who would benefit from that expertise, making providing referrals much easier.

3. **Event Marketing.** Tailor events to clients and prospects who are within the team's niche market. This makes it easier to get existing clients to invite their colleagues and friends that share the same profession or stage of life.

4. **Right Place—Right People.** Niche marketing is especially effective when using the direct approach. It is compelling when an FA team member approaches an affluent friend or family member and offers expertise that is specific to the occupation or stage of life of that individual. This is especially effective when the individual's current advisor does not possess that expertise, which will most often be the case.

5. **Assets Away.** When an affluent client fits within the team's niche the FA team members can make a compelling case as to why that client should have all of their assets with the team.

6. **Prospect Pipeline.** As I mentioned earlier, affluent individuals are drawn to financial advisors who specialize in their perceived unique financial circumstances. It is also easier to provide strong references with industry leaders that the advisor is currently working with.

Branding

The team needs to make the world aware of their specialization in a niche market; otherwise they are not leveraging this strategy to its full and considerable potential. Most advisory teams do not have marketing experience or expertise, but in this case they don't need to have either. Take the expertise you have and let the world know about it. Branding can be either formal or informal, and the following strategies are examples of each:

Formal
- Team's website
- LinkedIn profile of each individual team member
- Marketing material
- Team's value proposition
- Articles written within trade publications serving the niche market
- Sponsorship of events and membership in associations within the niche market
- Ads placed in local trade journals within the niche market

Informal
- Client referral conversations
- Social conversations
- Spreading word of mouth within the niche market
- Professional referral conversations

Team Accountability

Niche market updates, success stories, and challenges should be shared during the team marketing meetings.

The niche market strategy is really an enhancement to all the other acquisition strategies. When utilized it can turbocharge the other strategies, making them more productive. The best answer a financial advisory team can provide when an affluent prospect asks, "Why should I invest my million dollars with you?" is "*Because our team has a division in our practice that specializes and has experience with the unique and complex financial issues that people in your profession have.*"

THE MARKETING MEETING

The team marketing meeting is the "glue" that ties together all the acquisition strategies. It is the foundation from which the marketing division is built and maintained. I recommend that teams hold a regular marketing meeting that is focused on the implementation of these acquisition strategies. This marketing meeting keeps each team member accountable to the acquisition strategies. It also serves as an opportunity to provide recognition to individual team members who have had success, and a venue to track acquisition results.

The frequency of the team marketing meeting is a matter of team preference. There are three recommendations that I could make—any of which are acceptable:

1. A portion of each weekly team meeting is dedicated to marketing for least fifteen minutes.
2. Twice a month for thirty minutes as a separate meeting
3. A separate monthly meeting, typically for sixty minutes

If the team acquisition meeting is part of the weekly team meeting then it is more practical to review just one or two of the strategies, and the pipeline might be reviewed in one or two weekly meetings a month.

The agenda should be simple and disciplined:

- Reminder of the agreed upon goals for assets and new affluent clients for the year, along with quarterly target if appropriate (senior team leader)
- Review of results and recognition opportunity
- Reminder of motivation and the importance of achieving the marketing division goals (senior team leader)

- Review of each committed acquisition strategy—progress, challenges, feedback, and questions (each team member contributes)
- Review of the prospect pipeline by each FA team member
- Event calendar review
- Review of any other items of attention ensuring that each team member is able to provide feedback and input on how to improve the acquisition strategies

MARKETING CHECKLIST

❏ Have a referral process for identifying the team's loyal clients and having one meaningful in-person referral conversation with each loyal and highly satisfied client.

❏ Follow the recommended five-step approach to build a professional referral network.

❏ Follow the five recommended principles for successful event marketing.

❏ Each team member list twenty-five affluent personal acquaintances that they would like as clients but never approached and apply one of the three recommended transition strategies.

❏ Follow the recommended four-part asset away strategy.

❏ Build the team's prospect pipeline to twenty-five per team member and follow the guidelines outlined on managing the pipeline.

❏ Commit to a specialization and position it as a division of the team that specializes in (niche market). Follow the guidelines in developing a niche market plan.

❏ Develop a team value proposition that answers the question, Why should I invest my assets with you?

❏ Have a team marketing meeting following the recommended guidelines.

11

Developing Processes

There are two major drivers of team leverage: people and process. I have reviewed the leverage of people throughout the earlier chapters, and I believe it represents the biggest team lever. However, a close second is the leverage of process. In order for a team to maximize their productivity, they need to create scalability, and the only way to achieve this is to have a process-based practice.

The highest-functioning teams are process-based in terms of each function of their business, and without a doubt it is a team best practice. In fact, the more successful the teams the more processes they have in place. Among the teams I interviewed or researched were the top three teams in one of the largest wire house firms, and each of those three teams epitomized a process-based practice: Each had established processes for all of the team's functions. The most productive teams are process based, enabling them to be more efficient, providing scale and capacity to focus on the activities that drive growth.

Two examples of the power of process are the assembly line and a doctor's office. One of the most significant triggers that moved the American workforce from an agricultural to an industrial economy was the assembly line. Henry Ford realized that to sell a lot of cars, they had to be affordable. If each car was built separately its retail price would be higher than the average American could afford. Necessity is the mother of invention, and Henry Ford created the assembly line that enabled cars to be mass produced, where each worker only addressed one process, making it possible for multiple cars to be built at the same time. The result was that cars became much more affordable and could be produced more quickly. The assembly line concept was adopted by many industries both in manufacturing and service industries.

I have always been impressed by how medical professionals have created a process-based practice which contributes to their efficiency and productivity. When I make an appointment to see my doctor I call his office and get in touch with a scheduler. This person oversees the doctor's schedule and provides instructions as to any preparation I must do in advance of my appointment. Once it gets close to the appointment, I receive an email confirming the date, time, and preparation needed. When I show up for my appointment I am asked to show my insurance card and update a medical questionnaire. A nurse then greets me and gets me weighed, measured, and blood pressure taken. I sit in a room and my file is placed outside the door. The doctor quickly reviews my file before entering the room. He then asks me the same questions and does the same tests. He attends to my medical needs, provides a prescription or referrals to other specialists, and my file is given to the receptionist when I leave. Sometimes I have to go to a lab and to get blood work drawn. A report is generated to my doctor and either he or his nurse calls me with the results and next steps if needed. The entire process from start to finish typically takes one or two hours, and yet the doctor's involvement is merely fifteen to twenty minutes. I am charged $200 for the office visit. This process-based practice enables the doctor to see up to 20 patients a day, generating $4,000 in revenues for five hours of his time.

Whenever I work with a new team, I always ask if the team practice resembles a doctor's office. How they answer that question gives me a baseline of how much work needs to be done in order to create a process-based practice. Many of the teams I work with do not have processes in place, and every day they are reinventing the wheel. This is the epitome of inefficiency. However, once we can put processes into place, the team sees immediately how much better they work, and how much more successful they can be.

PROCESS BEST PRACTICE EXAMPLE: SEGMENTATION

Although this process takes time to establish up front, once developed and implemented it ensures a high-quality client experience, time savings for the FA, and a high level of efficiency. The following is an example of how to develop a thoughtful and detailed process for segmentation of the team's clients. This example should serve as a guide for not only segmentation but also for establishing individual processes within your team's practice.

Step 1: Establish that fifty clients is the ideal number of households that each FA should work with, and set a maximum limit of a hundred households per advisor. These are the guardrails for the team's segmentation practice.

Step 2: Each FA team member should have a divesture strategy for those households that exceed her limit or are below her minimum. A relationship manager can take over the responsibility for the team's smaller clients.

Step 3: Client contact frequency needs to be established and followed for each of these client relationships. The frequency will depend on the size of the relationship.

Step 4: Determine the type and the frequency of interactions that FA team partners need to have with clients they have assigned to the relationship manager. I recommend thirty minutes during each RM annual client review.

Step 5: Develop a script for FA team members to use when transitioning a client to the RM.

Step 6: Determine what preparation needs to be done prior to each client contact and review. Have an administrative member of the team prepare the necessary checklists and have them ready in advance of the review.

Step 7: Determine how both formal and informal contacts will be made and assign the scheduling responsibility to an administrative member of the team. I recommend informal monthly contact calls and quarterly reviews scheduled in advance.

Step 8: Write up notes and reviews after each contact is made, and assign any follow-up tasks to an administrative member of the team.

Step 9: Create and maintain files of these notes, which can then be reviewed prior to the next client meeting. This file includes notes, a personal profile on the client, action steps completed, and financial products and services that the client should be exposed to. The file should also include growth opportunities such as referrals, event invitations, and assets held away that the FA will refer to throughout the year.

Step 10: Establish time blocking for FAs for both proactive client monthly contacts and reviews depending on the predetermined frequency.

ORGANIZING TEAM PROCESSES

When I help teams organize and develop processes, I go back to the four divisions that I referenced in Chapter 4 when we discussed roles and responsibilities. Every successful business has a product division, a service division, a marketing division, and a human resource division.

A team needs to determine which processes they currently have, and which ones they need to develop and organize by these divisions.

This chapter provides a list of recommended processes the team should consider. It is not an all-inclusive list; additional processes could be included based on the type of services the team provides.

MARKETING DIVISION PROCESSES

For more details on the following marketing division processes, please refer to Chapter 10.

- **Referrals.** Implementing a consistent proactive referral process is the most productive strategy for acquisition of new affluent clients.

- **Professional Referral Network.** Teams that are motivated to grow their professional referral network need to develop a process in which they get permission from their clients to contact clients' CPAs and attorneys, meet with them regularly, and stay in touch with them on a consistent basis to build the requisite like and trust relationship.

- **Event Marketing.** Implement the 10 x10 event marketing process, following up on prospects within forty-eight hours, and have 50 percent of participants be prospects. Schedule the events a year in advance.

- **Assets Held Away.** The team needs to develop a process to identify their clients' assets held away, keep track of those away assets, and develop and implement strategies to bring them under the team's management.

- **Right Place—Right People.** Each FA partner should develop a list of at least twenty-five personal relationships that have acquisition potential and commit to one of the three transition strategies outlined in the marketing division chapter. The team needs to develop a process to transition these affluent personal relationships into prospects and eventually into clients.

- **Prospect Pipeline.** The team's pipeline needs to be built to twenty-five per FA team member. Treat these prospects as if they were the team's best clients through a monthly face or voice contact.

- **Niche Marketing.** Develop a niche market plan to incorporate a division or divisions within the team that specialize in an occupation or stage of life. The niche market plan should include: identification of the niche and expertise required, marketing activities to leverage the niche expertise, and branding to let the world know about the team's niche market expertise.

- **Pitch Book.** The team should develop a pitch book template to be used for prospect meetings. The pitch book should have a standard format that can be customized to the individual prospect situation. A pitch book is a presentation that highlights the team members, the team's wealth management process, its value proposition, and its specializations.

- **Value Proposition.** Develop a value proposition and be able to articulate it depending on the circumstances. Have a shorter condensed version and an expanded version.

- **Marketing Meeting.** The team partners need to meet at least monthly to review the prospecting activities and results achieved in the past and set goals for the future. Each partner needs to share their results and activities since the last meeting and the pipeline needs to be reviewed.

SERVICE DIVISION PROCESSES

- **Client Contact.** The team should develop a standardized process for the FA members to contact their top fifty client relationships. My recommendation is an 8/3/1 system—which is a monthly contact organized in the following way:

8 monthly informal touches to check in with clients (typically fifteen minutes)

3 formal quarterly reviews, if possible one done in person (typically thirty to forty-five minutes)

1 annual review, which also serves as the fourth quarter review. These should be done in person. (typically sixty to ninety minutes)

- **Documentation.** The team should standardize documentation for client contacts, meetings, and reviews. Documentation should occur immediately after every client contact. Documentation is invaluable for the FA to reference in future contacts, as well as for compliance and DOL requirements.

- **Personal Stakeholder Touches.** To develop loyal clients the team needs to incorporate personal touches or Wow moments of service. These touches should be institutionalized as processes. The non-FAs can administer them on the behalf of the FAs. Examples could include the following:

  Anniversary: Acknowledge when the client started the relationship with the advisor.

  Random acts of kindness: Look for opportunities to acknowledge special occasions and events that occur in the clients' lives.

  Most special day: Know the most special day in the client's life and acknowledge and recognize that every year.

  Financial milestones: Acknowledge and recognize when clients achieve financial milestones such as retirement, kids graduating from college, mortgages being paid off, and other important financial goals achieved.

  Events: Invite the client and spouse to a fun intimate event at least annually.

- **Onboarding.** Developing and implementing a first-ninety-day onboarding checklist to ensure that the new affluent client has a world-class experience. This sets the stage for the development of a loyal client by underpromising and overdelivering. Examples for an onboarding checklist could include:

  - ❏ Ensure that all transfer and new-account paperwork is completed and processed in a timely manner.
  - ❏ Have the sales associate assigned to the new client; make an introductory call within forty-eight hours of the account being opened.
  - ❏ Hold an introductory call with team members who will be involved in the client relationship.
  - ❏ Send a thank-you card and an investment-related book: we recommend Benjamin Graham's *The Intelligent Investor, The Warren Buffet Way,* or Jeremy Siegel's *Stocks for the Long Run.*
  - ❏ Review the first and second month's statements with the new client.
  - ❏ Make two proactive contacts during each of the first two months.
  - ❏ Have the manager place a welcome call.

- **Client profile.** Developing a written profile for each FA team member's top fifty clients is highly recommended. This profile is designed to uncover and keep track of clients' personal information. This is the basis for the personal touches and Wow moments. Examples of information obtained could include most special day of client's life, children and grandchildren, outside interests, passions, and charitable inclinations.

- **Incoming call response.** Every non-FA team member who answers incoming calls should have a standardized script. This ensures professionalism and the ability to screen calls for FAs.

- **Proactive service call.** This process epitomizes proactive service by the administrative team members. It is an outgoing call to offer help to clients before they bring up problems, challenges, or issues. It's recommended that each top client receives two proactive service calls a year.

- **Problem resolution.** The team should establish a problem resolution process. I recommend the "communicate and elevate" process. If a client brings up a problem, it is assigned to a member of the team to resolve. If the resolution is delayed it should be elevated to a more senior member while communicating to the client the status of the problem's resolution.

- **Client segmentation.** The team should create a process to identify the best clients of the practice and ensure that they receive the best service possible, the most frequent contact and implementation of Wow moments, and at least a ten hour a year time commitment from their FA. Please refer to the "Process Best Practice Example: Segmentation" provided earlier in this chapter for more details on this process.

THE OFFERING/PRODUCT DIVISION

The wealth management process is developed and implemented to guide the FA clients to reach their financial goals. There are a number of wealth management processes that best practicing teams incorporate into their practice. The wealth management process can be organized around the five cornerstones of a world-class offering:

Discovery

The team should incorporate three components into their discovery process. The discovery meeting should be done in person and include both the decisionmaker and the significant other whenever possible. The majority of the meeting should be devoted to gaining a full understanding of the client's circumstances using a questionnaire template that serves as a guide. The third component is making sure you cover and understand the client's risk tolerance and make sure it is realistic as it relates to the client's goals.

Client Reviews

The process for each quarterly review should be structured to include seven components:

1. *Opening.* Build rapport and go over agenda.
2. *Update.* Update information on the client to include goals, balance sheet, and risk assessment.
3. *Performance review.* Review both portfolio performance and progress toward goals.
4. *Market perspective.* Communicate current outlook on markets and impact on client's portfolio.
5. *Wealth management planning.* Go over estate planning, risk management (insurance), and lending (during the annual review).
6. *Summary.* Review what was covered during the session and agree upon next action steps.
7. *Closing Question.* Open the floor to any conversation the client wants to bring up.

Wallet Expansion

There is a 100 percent wallet share formula that I use to help FA teams build processes to increase their client's wallet share. The formula is **P + D + E = 100 (wallet share).**

P Position with every client during every annual review that it is in the client's best interest to have all of their financial assets with one advisor who develops and implements a financial plan with the intent of the client reaching his financial goals.

D Discover all the assets and financial products and services that the client has away from the financial advisor. This can and should be done through the financial planning process.

E Expose the client during monthly contacts to those products and services that the client should utilize that the team provides.

Goal-Based Investing

Best practicing teams recognize that what's most important to their affluent clients is the successful achievement of financial goals. One of the top advisors explained it well, *"A goal is an unfunded liability and our team's objective is to develop a plan to fund those liabilities, enabling our clients to reach their financial goals within an acceptable timeframe."* The following are the best practices of goal-based investing:

- The deep discovery process is the basis from which the clients' goals are established.
- The team's objective is to determine the client's minimum, desired, and aspirational goals and develop a plan to achieve them.
- Develop a baseline of all assets including those held away so that they can be included in goal-based reviews.
- Evaluation of the team is based on the achievement of realistic goals, not short-term market performance based on an arbitrary index.
- Manage expectations of clients and remind them of those realistic expectations throughout the process.

Investment Discipline

Many of the highest-functioning teams have developed a well-thought-through investment process. Their investment processes could be summarized into seven characteristics:

1. They have a clearly defined, disciplined investment process that can be easily explained to all prospects and clients.
2. They educate their clients about their investment process in order to build client advocacy.
3. They use asset allocation as both a risk-management and a performance-building tool.
4. They believe having a macro view of the economic landscape is a necessity.
5. They have high conviction investment strategies and use model portfolios to bring scale and credibility to their practice.
6. They don't chase investment fads and they take a stand against extremes.
7. They view performance reporting as a critical tool in maintaining client communication.

HUMAN RESOURCES DIVISION

The following are examples of human resources processes that have been referenced in more detail in the preceding chapters "Assigning Roles and Responsibilities," "Performance Reviews and Measurements," "Team Compensation," and "Best Practices for Hiring":

- **Team meetings.** Three core team meeting venues that best practicing teams use include the daily stand up meeting, weekly meeting, and annual strategic meeting.

- **Written job descriptions.** Formal descriptions for each team member ensure everyone is clear on what their responsibilities are and who they are accountable to.

- **Performance reviews.** These are held semiannually and focus on the three to five high-priority measurable tasks that each team member has been assigned and that are included in their job descriptions with a controller measuring and rating how they performed these high-priority jobs.

- **Compensation.** This is based on three parts—base salary, a performance bonus, and a team bonus. This compensation recognizes the highest-performing and most-productive employees.

- **Hiring.** Do a thoughtful analysis of the team's hiring needs and what are the most important roles to add. Develop a sourcing, interviewing, and training process for new hires to ensure the highest probability of their success.

It is important to remind the reader that while we believe the processes outlined in this chapter are essential, they do not constitute an all-encompassing list of all the processes a team should employ. Rather, they are all core processes that should be included in the team's practices.

PROCESS GAP ANALYSIS

At Altius Learning, we have created a tool for developing and improving team processes. This Process Gap Analysis is designed to both identify processes that should be developed, and to evaluate and rate existing processes. The Process Gap Analysis is broken into the four divisions that we recommended in Chapter 4, describing the processes that we believe all financial advisory teams should maintain. See Appendix B for a "Process Gap Analysis Form" you can use.

Next to each recommended process, rate your existing processes on a scale of 1 to 10, with 10 being the highest rating. The target rating column is designed to be aspirational; how important the rating is will indicate what the target rating should be. As an example, in the marketing division the referral process target might be 10 while the professional referral network might be a 5. These target ratings can be adjusted every year if the team's priorities change. Use this tool to assign the responsibility for developing or implementing one process to each team member if there is a gap between the current and target rating, or if a particular process doesn't currently exist. Set a completion date for improving an existing process or for the development of a new one.

PROCESSES CHECKLIST

- ❑ Organize the processes you have in place by the four essential divisions.
- ❑ Use the "Process Gap Analysis Form" (Appendix B) to organize and evaluate the current and needed processes for the team.
- ❑ Identify the processes the team needs but does not have in place by division.
- ❑ Develop processes you would like to have but don't currently have in place.
- ❑ Implement those new processes and assign responsibility for oversight to a team member.
- ❑ Review and update team processes to ensure they are implemented and functioning at a satisfactory level.

12

Team Leadership

have spent the majority of my career in leadership positions in the financial services industry and have witnessed firsthand what a positive impact good leadership can make. I have also seen all too often how poor leadership can hurt an organization. The highest-functioning teams have good leadership, because without it a team will never be a highly functioning team.

The challenge most financial advisory teams face is that the characteristics that make a successful financial advisor are not necessarily the same characteristics that make good leaders. In many cases they are opposing characteristics. Many of the most successful FAs that I have worked with are goal-oriented, achievement-driven individuals with strong egos. These are not necessarily leadership attributes. Great leaders put the team ahead of their own needs, are empathetic, and are very emotionally aware.

Very few financial advisors have had leadership training or have colleagues in leadership positions to learn from. When I was groomed to be a manager at Merrill Lynch, I had to participate in a formal leadership training program, where I could learn from instructors as well as from my colleagues and where I had the opportunity to be mentored by a number of great leaders.

Most financial advisors enter this career because they want to build a successful advisory practice. In most cases they are entrepreneurs, not corporate leaders. I have had many FAs tell me that they have no interest in management, the politics of the office, or the paperwork and other assorted hassles they assume come with leadership. The irony is that as FAs become more successful they have to build teams to reach their full potential.

THE MILLION-DOLLAR FINANCIAL ADVISOR TEAM

I strongly believe that even without specific leadership experience, training, or role models, successful FAs can acquire the leadership skills needed to lead their teams effectively. In fact, they already use these leadership skills working with their best clients. The truth is that the best financial advisors are leaders for their clients; if they can connect the leadership skills they already demonstrate with their clients to their team they will be the leaders that their teams need them to be. The following are examples of how great financial advisors apply leadership principles daily with their clients:

- Provide vision through financial planning
- Make hard decisions and guide clients through volatile and uncertain markets
- Communicate with their clients frequently, reminding them of the financial plan and the importance of following it
- Provide empathy by becoming involved in clients' lives, and helping them achieve their hopes and dreams while balancing their risk tolerance
- Holding themselves and their clients accountable to the discipline required to reach their financial goals
- Always putting the clients' interests in front of their own, and demonstrating ethical behavior at all times
- Serve as good listeners by hearing their client's needs, fears, and dreams, and helping clients achieve goals that are tailored to these issues
- Delegate operational work to their administrative team members and hold them accountable
- Prioritize their most important tasks

DELEGATING LEADERSHIP TO JUNIOR
TEAM MEMBERS

I have also seen examples of senior FAs delegating the team leadership role to a more junior member of the team who either has the needed leadership skills or is willing to assume leadership and develop the necessary leadership skills to do so. A good example of this is with Taylor Glover's team.

Taylor was Merrill Lynch's number one producer when I worked with him, and over time he built a great team. Taylor was an effective leader but his passion was attaining new clients and spending time with his biggest clients. Taylor's most valuable contribution to the team was the relationships he had with the team's best clients and his business development. As a result, he had the foresight to appoint Art as the team leader. Art was a natural leader, and had leadership experience as an executive in the banking industry. Art involved Taylor in the most important decisionmaking, but was responsible for the day-to-day leadership of the team. In essence, he became the team's COO. Art was responsible for ensuring the team investment process was followed, for developing and implementing the team's service model, for hiring and firing team employees, for employee performance reviews, for settling disputes among team members, and for determining compensation of team employees. Taylor was involved in many of these decisions, but Art implemented them.

CORE TEAM LEADERSHIP PRINCIPLES

It's beyond the scope of this book to cover in depth how to be an effective leader. However, the best team practices we've discussed throughout this book can be applied to developing excellent leadership skills. If team leaders utilize these team best practices, they can become effective team leaders.

Attract, Train, and Retain Talent

The highest priority for any team leader is attracting the best talent, developing that talent, and retaining talent by creating happy and successful employees. Assigning the right level of accountability, providing fair compensation, and bestowing frequent recognition are the cornerstones of retention of talent. These team best practices were covered primarily in "Best Practices for Hiring" (Chapter 8). If a team leader develops the processes outlined in the hiring chapter they will have a great team. As Sir Richard Branson has said:

"Train someone so well they can leave and trust them well enough that they don't want to."

Accountability

Accountability means overseeing roles and responsibilities, performance reviews, and compensation. By creating clear, written responsibilities for each team member, your team will know what their jobs entail and the basis for which they will be reviewed. Compensation must fairly reflect the accomplishment of those roles and responsibilities—with generous compensation being paid for high performance. A team leader must treat team members fairly through compensation and recognition, and must demonstrate a no tolerance policy for poor performance. Fair does not mean equal, and the best performers must be given generous compensation and recognition, while poor performers must face consequences. If this balance is not maintained then low morale and turnover of good performers will result. These team best practices were covered in the sections on roles and responsibility (Chapter 4), performance reviews (Chapter 5), and compensation (Chapter 6).

Integrity

Team members need to be able to trust their leaders. A team leader's words and actions must always align. Team integrity starts at the top, and the team leader must be a role model. Team members watch how the team leader treats their clients and other team members. Any deviation from the gold standard of behavior that is not trustworthy or consistent is noticed, and sends a message that poor behavior is tolerated.

A team leader has to have zero tolerance for a lack of integrity from any team member. A team is only as good as its weakest link, and having a team member demonstrate unethical behavior is a reflection on the entire team. This is especially true in an industry that is based on trust.

Vision

Everyone wants to find purpose and meaning in their job. The team leader provides leadership by being a big dreamer, being capable of taking action to accomplish those dreams, and by inspiring the team to do the same. She must be able to provide and articulate a vision for the team that inspires and motivates all the team members to achieve that shared vision. Sharing a vision also keeps the team focused on the most important activities and gives them clear goals to work toward.

The team leader should work with the team on developing a business plan that clearly outlines how the team vision will be achieved, communicates progress toward the vision, and holds team members accountable for their role in implementing the business plan. This team best practice was covered in the vision section (Chapter3).

Communication

No leadership principle is more important than maintaining frequent communication from the team leader to the staff, and being open to feedback from team members. As an effective team leader it is essential to be a good listener. The team leader must be willing to encourage team members to challenge his ideas and direction. This skillset can be one of the most challenging aspects for successful FAs who are in the team leader role. While listening is very important in their role as financial advisors, many FAs are not good at it in the context of their team role.

The best team leaders encourage an open-door policy and welcome team members' input, feedback, and challenges—understanding that two-way communication makes the team better. The team leader must be involved in (if not lead) all team meetings. The team leader must incorporate and reinforce formal team communication through daily and weekly strategic team meetings. This team best practice was covered in the communication chapter (Chapter 7).

Decisionmaking

To be an effective team leader it is essential to be a good decisionmaker. A good decisionmaker comes to conclusions quickly, and incorporates the points of view of other team members.

I have learned through experience that as a leader, you are incapable of making all the right decisions and you will never be 100 percent certain that your decision is right before you make it. If you wait until you are 100 percent sure your decision is right you will never make a decision, which can then paralyze a team. Leaders must also accept that some of their decisions will turn out wrong despite best intentions; they need to accept the consequences of these decisions. Great leaders can learn from their mistakes and move forward.

One of my favorite quotes that reflects good decisionmaking is from a gentleman that had to make instant decisions with enormous consequences to his team—Peyton Manning, one of the all-time great quarterbacks: *"You can be a warrior or a worrier—a great leader makes decisions without flip flopping, vacillation, or second guessing."*

One of the most valuable leadership lessons I learned was to encourage input from the members of my management team. By getting multiple points of view that either validated or challenged my thought process, the decisions I made were always better. Just as important, I had confidence in them. I encourage team leaders to follow the same process and get multiple points of view from other team members before making important decisions.

Delegation

By nature, financial advisors do not like to give up control. They typically feel a deep sense of responsibility to their clients, and realize their livelihood and that of their clients is tied to them doing a good job. Because of that sense of responsibility, it becomes hard to give up control to other team members. However, a team leader will never realize the full benefit of a team without effectively delegating tasks.

The team leader must ensure their team is built to handle all of the non-big three tasks that FAs can pass on to someone else. The team leader should also be a role model for effective delegation. This team best practice was covered in "Assigning Roles and Responsibilities" (Chapter 4).

Prioritization

The team leader needs to consistently remind the team of their most important priorities, based on the team vision and business plan. Without the emphasis and reinforcement of the team's priorities it can be easy for team members to get distracted by the endless low-priority tasks that present themselves every day. Examples of high priorities include the acquisition of new affluent clients and assets, delivering world-class service, implementing a thoughtful and disciplined investment process, frequent and quality client communication, and the segmentation of clients within the practice (ensuring the majority of time and attention is spent with the team's best clients). These priorities can be communicated during team meetings.

Maintaining a Positive Attitude

The best leaders are positive role models. There will always be difficult challenges, tough markets, loss of key clients, compliance issues, and human resource challenges. The team leader must be resolute in facing those challenges and be a positive force within the team so that the other team members can look to them when real leadership is needed.

Over the years, I have learned that a positive outlook inspires, while pessimism discourages. There were many times when I felt overwhelmed by difficult challenges and circumstances but I learned I needed to keep those negative emotions to myself and put on my best game face to give my management team members the inspiration they needed to work through those challenges. In other words, I needed to lead by example and provide optimistic leadership even in the face of difficult challenges.

The good news is the most successful FAs are optimists by nature. This is one of the easier leadership principles for most team leaders to adopt from their dealings with clients.

COMPENSATING A TEAM LEADER

An effective team leader is essential to the team's success and a good return on the team's investment. As the team is being formed it should be determined in advance who the team leader will be, along with the leader's responsibilities and compensation. In a vertical team structure the team leader is typically the senior partner.

The most common compensation for a team leader is an increased team pool equity split to compensate for the time and energy required to be effective. This is not necessarily a large split increase, but enough to make the team leadership role worthwhile.

LEADERSHIP CHECKLIST

- ❑ Do you take time to inspire team members through your energy and commitment to the team vision?
- ❑ Do you focus your time and attention on the team's highest priorities and those things that are controllable?
- ❑ Do you hold yourself and other team members to the highest standards of performance?
- ❑ Do you encourage input from other team members? Are you willing to accept challenges to your ideas?
- ❑ Do you set the highest standards for new team members? Does the team provide a high level of training?
- ❑ Do you have accountability measurements? Do you recognize and compensate for good and outstanding performance?
- ❑ Do you have a positive outlook? Are you resilient after setbacks?
- ❑ Have you shared the team values? Do you hold everyone accountable to following them?
- ❑ Have you created a strong team culture that emphasizes excellence and is client centric?
- ❑ Do you lead by example, doing what you expect your team members to do?
- ❑ Do you have zero tolerance for a lack of integrity from any team member?
- ❑ Have you established a team vision? Do you communicate it frequently to other team members?
- ❑ Are you willing to take risks in order to grow and improve the team? Are you willing to reinvent yourself and the team?
- ❑ Do you treat others the way you want to be treated and show other team members that you care?
- ❑ Are you committed to self-improvement? Do you foster a learning and self-improvement team environment?

❑ Are you willing to make hard decisions in a timely way? Are you a warrior or a worrier?

❑ Do you emphasize team success rather than individual success?

13

Highly Functioning Team Case Studies

T his chapter is designed to highlight some of the highest-functioning teams in our industry. These featured teams were among those that I interviewed for this book, and many of the team best practices were drawn from these interviews.

I have found that some of the most valuable insights that financial advisors can glean are from industry leaders and leaders of highly functioning teams. Use these profiles as a tool so that you can emulate selected practices and improve the functioning of your own team.

RICHARD: **HIRING IS A HIGH PRIORITY**

Structure—Horizontal

Richard's team consists of four advisors (including himself) and three client associates. Of the four advisors, three are traditional financial advisors and one is a chief investment manager; he has a CFA. The four financial advisor partners manage client relationships and are responsible for business development.

The partners cover for each other as needed and their clients know that they are serviced by the entire team. This reinforces what Richard considers a key message—the team has depth, expertise, and a diversity of experience.

This is a horizontal team and the two founding partners each have a 33 percent split. The remaining two partners' splits are 20 percent and 10 percent, which is based on their experience and the legacy business they brought in when they joined the team.

The team services a total of 150 client relationships that generate approximately $5 million.

Richard believes that "advisors have to have a manageable business, and the team needs to define what is manageable." He believes that a manageable number of clients is not a specific number but rather a range—which he defines as "guardrails." He was clear that high net worth clients with more complicated needs take more time and as a result there are limitations on how many of these relationships a single advisor can work with.

While Richard agreed that fifty high net worth households is a good guideline for each individual financial advisor, he also believes an investment associate with a CFP could provide scale to the partners. His plan is to hire multiple investment associates whose responsibilities include the planning functions of the team clients. These could be former CPAs or attorneys, and are in a salaried position. This type of team member enables the other partners to work with more clients because all of the planning work can be delegated. He believes that in the future, his team will have fewer partners and more salaried investment associate professionals.

Vision

Richard shared that the team has spent countless hours looking at revenue models and charting out their goals for future growth. His team uses a five-year timeframe for their team business plan. They focus on business growth, million + new households, and new assets. The business plan also emphasizes accountability: not just goals but who is accountable for reaching those goals. In addition to tactical goals they also believe in being accountable for goals like attending team meetings, being good team players, and maintaining work standards. They have focused a lot of time and energy on developing a thoughtful succession plan. Richard believes that having a succession plan is important to communicate with their best clients and he finds the team's clients are reassured that they have one.

Communication

The team holds one formal team meeting a week and one quarterly meeting. The weekly meeting is one hour long and focuses on the calendar, pending issues, and pipeline review. The quarterly meeting is focused on accountability and the metrics of their business, comparing the results to the goals set for the year.

Accountability

Richard believes that one of the team's highest priorities is to set expectations for each individual team member and expectations for the team, which drives accountability. He also believes that everyone on the team should have definable and controllable metrics—from support staff to partners. The FA partners need to be accountable to bring in new business, which is the only way they will receive more equity ownership and a higher team split. Richard's view is that if an FA doesn't bring in new business than a salaried employee can replace that FA—rainmaking is the difference between being a partner and an employee.

The team has two formal performance reviews for all support employees every year. These performance reviews include all aspects of the job: work ethic, attitude, and the performance of controllable and high-priority tasks and activities that they have been assigned.

Roles and Responsibilities

The team partners all have joint responsibilities in addition to being producers. One partner is responsible for human resources, another serves as the CFO for the team, and Richard is the CEO, responsible for human resources as well as the senior relationship manager for the team's largest clients.

As mentioned earlier, Richard is a strong believer in the investment associate position for handling all aspects of the planning process. This employee schedules client reviews, reviews their past plan in advance of the review, and gets everything ready for the review session, including setting up the agenda. The associate also does all the follow-up work after the review. The investment associate is responsible for stock option analysis and the metrics on the practice. As an example, they review the contact management system and produce a list of clients that haven't been contacted in the past ninety days.

Compensation

The team pays their senior client associates between $75,000 and $95,000, which includes a base salary and bonuses. New client associates typically start in the $60,000 to $65,000 range. The investment associate position starts at $85,000 and over time can make up to $125,000. The team also has an annual partner compensation meeting where equity splits are reviewed to determine each partner's split, based on their contributions for the past year, and whether they want to work less in the coming year (in which case their split would be lowered).

MIKE: THE IMPORTANCE OF LEADERSHIP

Structure—Vertical

Mike is the senior partner of a team that includes four other members. The team shares one client associate who also acts as the chief operating officer, and handles all of the clients' administrative requests—wire transfers, questions about statements, and other administrative and operational issues. The other three team members are financial analysts: Two are CFAs and the last is working on getting his CFA. According to Mike the "team's DNA" is strongly investment-centric. The reason the team has three analysts and only one client associate is that they work with a limited number of ultra-high net worth families, and the administrative burden is relatively light. Mike's team does $5 million on a billion in assets under management.

Hiring

When hiring new team members Mike focuses on individuals who are looking to make a long-term commitment to the team. He appreciates the value of stability both for him and for the team's clients.

Mike looks to hire people who have experience beyond a first job. Mike believes you want to hire people who really want the job—it's not a plan B job until something better comes along. He also believes that it helps to hire people who have geographic ties to the area and stability in their lives. All of his current team members own homes and have families.

Roles and Responsibilities

Mike places a high priority on his financial analysts having a broad skillset so they can cover for each other when necessary; he doesn't want to have critical tasks that only one person can do. Mike has his financial analysts working on different client projects and working in different functional areas in the practice to ensure that knowledge is institutionalized and shared. The financial analysts interact with the team's clients on a consistent basis. Mike shared an example of meeting with a CEO of a public company. While he took the lead role he had two of the analysts sit in on the meeting. Mike wanted to build this relationship from the beginning so that when he is out of the office the client feels comfortable working with the analysts.

Team Offering

Of all the best practicing teams that I interviewed none were more focused on making sure there is a good fit between the prospective client and the team than Mike's. The team is highly focused on their mission and understanding who they are, what they do, and what clients they can add value for, rather than looking to just generate business.

While they have the capacity to add five to ten new ultra-high net worth families, if the fit isn't a good one they will pass on the opportunity. Mike feels that adding a client who doesn't fit with their practice is a waste of time, and he won't let that happen.

Leadership

Providing strong leadership for his team is a very high priority for Mike. Some of the leadership insights that Mike shared with me include:

- **Decisionmaking.** Problems don't solve themselves and they don't go away. If Mike has a problem with someone on the team—with performance, attitude, or not getting along with other team members—he addresses it right away. Otherwise, bad habits get formed and resentments build.

- **Right people.** If you have the wrong person on a small team that is disruptive, isn't a team player, or has an abrasive personality that person has to be removed as soon as possible. Mike used the following analogy, *"[My team] is like a river flowing downstream; you want the river to flow smoothly. Having the wrong person on the team is like having a big boulder in that river that all workflow needs flow around."*

- **High standards.** Mike believes in setting a higher standard for the team than the toughest client would set. He told me, "So I am the team's toughest client." As the team leader Mike sets the bar so high relative to the team's standards and quality control that even the toughest, most difficult, highest-expectation client isn't going to present a problem.

- **Clear mission.** Mike has a very clear mission statement and leverages and grooms the team in order to achieve that mission.

- **Keep it simple.** Mike doesn't believe this business is complicated, but it's difficult, requiring discipline, focus, and hard work. He focuses the team on achieving the mission and not getting distracted by busy work that takes away from the highest priorities of the team.

- **Hire well.** Don't compromise your hiring standards because you are in a hurry. Mike believes that patience is essential in hiring the right person. He admits his biggest hiring mistakes were made when he had to replace a team member and rushed to fill the spot. He also believes that when you bring in a new team member you have to emphasize the team mission and priorities, and make sure they are focused from day one on delivering that mission.

HAROLD: THE SINGLE MOST IMPORTANT TEAM PRACTICE IS COMMUNICATION

Structure—Horizontal

Harold is a senior partner with six other partners whose experience levels range from seven to forty years. The team has three investment associates: a 401k specialist, a fixed income specialist, and a relationship manager (assigned smaller accounts). The team also has a chief investment analyst and two assistants that support him. The team has four senior client associates who are responsible for servicing the team's clients and are each assigned to one or two of the team's partners. The team also has two junior client associates who support the senior client associates, for a total of six client associates. The junior client associates focus on preparation for client reviews, ensuring that the partners have all the reports and information they need for the reviews.

The team has two junior financial advisors that have not yet earned partner status, which is dependent on their ability to bring in new assets. They are the sons of the team's founding partners and must earn their future roles in the team's long-term succession plan.

The team also does situational partnering with two financial advisors who are not part of the team. This situational partnering occurs when a team partner sources a client below their million-dollar minimum. Harold's team has been pleased with these situational partnerships and splits the business with them 50/50 for the life of the relationship. They introduce these smaller opportunities to one of these two advisors by saying to these clients, *"We don't currently have the capacity to provide you the service you need, but we have someone on our team that does, and I would like to introduce you to them."*

This large team has evolved from the founding senior partners, Harold and Bill, who formed the team almost forty years ago. Harold worked with affluent individual clients and Bill had institutional experience when the two joined together; they are also brothers-in-law. Currently the team generates $18 million in production. It is the largest-producing team in their state and one of the largest at their major wire house firm. The partners target new clients with a $2 million minimum but continue to work with legacy clients who are in the million-dollar range. The team currently has sixty households that have over $10 million and six hundred relationships between $1 million and $10 million. This represents about eighty households for each of the seven partners.

Communication

Harold believes that the single most important practice for their team is communication. They organize team meetings around an 8:30 a.m. meeting that occurs every day except Thursday. On Monday, the entire team meets and reviews the weekly calendar (which is printed out), and any other items that have come up since the last meeting. Harold goes around the room and asks each team member for an update. The meeting on Monday is usually thirty minutes.

On Tuesday, it's the team investment committee, which consists of Harold, another senior partner, and the team's chief investment analyst. The chief investment analyst's job is to collate all of the investment news that they get and make sure the entire team is speaking with the same voice. He also runs the team's discretionary investment portfolios. The investment analyst and his junior analysts free up the seven partners from having to spend time on the research mechanics of the investment process.

The Wednesday meeting is designed for the partners to get together and review their prospect pipeline. The partners keep a running list of all the individuals they are prospecting. During the Wednesday meeting they talk about where they stand with each prospect, when the next contact is, review the potential of each opportunity and who is the best person to contact that prospect. According to Harold this Wednesday meeting "avoids having prospects falling through the cracks." Harold believes that the bigger the list the more their business will grow: "Their prospect pipeline is the leading indicator of the growth of the team." The Wednesday meetings are typically thirty minutes.

Friday's meeting focuses on highlighting victories from the past week. For example, the team discussed the fact that their fee-based number reached a record level for that month. They also discussed that one of their clients who is an assistant coach at a college level was just hired as a coach for the NFL. Additionally, they celebrated bringing in a new $3.5 million fee-based account. According to Harold, "the purpose of the Friday meeting is to drive the point that what we are doing is worth celebrating." The Friday meetings are typically fifteen minutes.

Additionally, the team has a partner meeting quarterly that takes approximately two hours, focuses on more strategic issues, and includes an open discussion on any issues that a partner wants to bring up. All told, these meetings take up less than two hours a week. This is a relatively small investment of time for the benefit that it provides that team. Team communication when well organized and structured does not need to take a great deal of time and is one of the best returns on investment that a team can make.

Job Description

The team requires that each nonpartner team member write their job description and what their highest priorities are for the coming year. Additionally, each nonpartner team member is required to include the extra things they are going to do to help the team, those that go above and beyond their job descriptions.

Accountability and Performance

Harold explained that his team focuses less on the individual team member performance than on the team performance and their contributions to the team. To quote Harold, "The thing I can't tolerate is when I hear someone brag about getting a new account. I always call them out and let them know that the team got the account—the FA didn't get it by himself." According to Harold, "It's like the elementary school report card when it says 'he or she works and plays well with others.'"

The team does semiannual performance reviews with the non-financial advisor team members, that are conducted by the partner that they support. The reviews are subjective and are based on contributions to the team, attitude, and team spirit. Harold explains that if a team member is underperforming the other team members put pressure on that member to raise her game or move on—peer pressure is powerful force.

Compensation

The two founding partners split the legacy business of $7 million 50/50. This was the business that they were producing prior to the other five partners joining the team. Every year the team has a partner compensation meeting and the splits are adjusted based on contributions on the non-legacy business. The founding partners are committed to fairness to the other partners and have been willing to give up their production split if it is deserved. Currently the two founding partners are each getting 22.5 percent of the total team's production.

The nonpartners are paid a salary and a subjective bonus that is determined by the seven partners at the end of the year. The senior client associates' total compensation ranges from $100,000 to $130,000. According to Harold, the investment associates make a "little more than that." The junior client associates typically make $40,000 to $50,000.

The budget for non-partner compensation is 11 percent of the team's compensation. This budget is in addition to the firm's base salaries. Each partner contributes to this budget based on business split. As an example, Harold gets a 22.5 percent split of the team's business and contributes 22.5 percent of the team compensation budget (22.5 percent of the total 11 percent team budget).

Vision and Reinvention

The team has a four-year vision on assets, multimillion clients, and business growth. They track their results "like a hawk." Their four-year goal is $25 million from their current level of $18 million.

This team never stops trying to get better and encourages a consistent reinvention process to enable that. Harold shared that five years ago the senior partners realized that if they wanted to double their business they had to change the way they did business—they had to reinvent themselves. This process led them to scale back the number of clients, hiring junior client associates to support their client associates, and a number of other changes that needed to be made. This reinvention paid off: The team's business doubled in five years. Harold believes that to reach the $25 million goal they need to go back through the reinvention process.

Leadership

Harold describes his leadership role as the team cheerleader. He believes he needs to be a positive role model, and no matter how he might feel he needs to project positive energy to the rest of the team. He promotes team spirit and the importance of a positive, can-do attitude.

Harold has passed the managing partner role to Ron, who has been with the team for twenty-one years and is forty-three years old. Harold feels Ron is closer in age to the majority of the nonpartner team members and can relate better to them.

One of the perks Harold offers is that the team sets a long-term goal, and if the team reaches it the entire team goes on a trip. Last year they reached their goal and went to Las Vegas, all expenses paid for four days. Past trips have been to Atlantis in the Bahamas, and if they reach the next big goal they will go to the Ritz Carlton in Puerto Rico.

CHARLES AND STEVE: MASTERS OF THE PROCESS

Structure: Horizontal

This is a horizontal team that is comprised of two senior partners, three client associates, an analyst, and a junior partner responsible for planning and next-generation clients. The team produces $8 million that is split evenly between Charles and Steve, with a small split going to the junior partner. They manage approximately $1.5 billion in assets and work with 130 total relationships.

As financial advisors, Charles and Steve are responsible for relationship management and business development. The three client associates have different responsibilities. The lead administrative CA helps with the onboarding of clients from new documents to cost basis to setting up credit cards. Another focuses on 144-concentrated stock, prepares client reviews, and manages the client contact management system. She keeps the partners appraised of significant events and information about their clients (such as where the client's kids go to school, what are the client's outside interests, their favorite charities).

The third client associate has a strong background in providing a world-class client experience: She worked in the high-end hospitality industry for eight years prior to joining the team. Her role is to provide a wonderful client experience day in and day out. As an example, every quarter she makes sure that the team's clients and their CPAs are emailed with their year-to-date investment income and year-to-date gains and losses.

The analyst facilitates all of the client plans, and has a lot of interaction with clients. When onboarding a client, the analyst reviews the financial plan questionnaire, re-verifying and understanding the client's goals, needs, and objectives. She then inputs and compiles the data and works with the partners to put together an investment proposal. She also does analysis on market-linked investments, mutual funds, hedge funds, and private equity.

The junior partner, Mark, is Charles's son. Mark has a CFP and provides oversight of the team's planning process. He is charged with millennial relationships and ensuring the team helps all the family members of their high net worth clients. He is also in charge of the team's syndicate and exchange funds. Over the long term the team would like Mark to look out for transitional wealth opportunities: when clients have big life changes he would alert the team to include merger and acquisition opportunities with existing and prospective clients.

Roles and Responsibilities

The team partners have complementary skills. The partners believe that each team member has a "genius" and they want to make sure they are in a position to add the genius to the cumulative offering of the team. Charles is a big picture thinker. He is a natural story-teller, and focuses on the fixed income strategy for the team. Steve, who has a CIMA, is responsible for restricted stock and stock option strategies for their clients and prospective clients.

The team believes that the partners, client associates, and analyst are interchangeable and all serve all the clients rather than being assigned specific clients. The client will interact with a team member depending on their needs. If it were a fixed income need they would speak with Charles; a stock option question would be directed to Steve. The same applies to the client associates—they interact with the client based on their expertise not because they were assigned that client.

Performance and Accountability

The partners do quarterly team member reviews and focus on their current roles and responsibilities and specific goals they have been assigned. Before the reviews the partners get together and share notes, observations, and experiences they have had with the employee. The partners do these reviews together, and they typically last thirty minutes. The following are some examples of questions covered during these reviews:

- How do you feel about your current roles and responsibilities and goals that have been set?
- Are there tasks you would like to do more of?
- Are there tasks you would like to do less of?
- Share client and team feedback on the team member.

Vision

The team has a playbook that is designed to achieve its long-term vision. The playbook doesn't change very much, but each year it is evaluated and fine-tuned as needed. The team goals include bringing in three to four clients a year that have at least $10 million, and they would like to divest 30 to 40 smaller clients to get their total relationships to 100 from the current level of 130. They would like to grow their business by 10 percent a year.

The partners believe the playbook shouldn't be focused just on business metrics but also on stress level, quality time with clients, and with the family. The team partners include their own personal goals in their playbook: how many fun activities (skiing, golf, fishing) will they do with their clients, how many Fridays can they take off, how often are they able to leave before 5:00 during the week, and how many vacation days will they take.

Compensation

All of the nonpartner members of the team get a percentage of the business as their bonus. This includes the four client associates and the analyst. The longer they are with the team the higher the percentage. Their base compensation is the firm's base salary and then the team has two other ways of paying them bonuses. First, they give their nonpartner team members 25 percent of any of the cash portion growth bonuses they receive from their firm. Second, they pay the nonpartner team members between 0.25 and 1.25 percent of the team's business. As an example, the most senior client associates and analyst make approximately $150,000. The partners budget 8 percent a year of their gross business to be paid to their employees. On $8 million that would be $640,000 in team compensation.

The partners believe their team members should be compensated at the highest levels for the industry. To quote Charles: "If you walk across the street and can make more than you currently make you are underpaid. If you walk across the street and make the same you are fairly paid. But if you walk across the street and can't get anywhere near what you make here, you are overpaid. I always want to be the highest paying team." Their commitment to their employees has resulted in a high level of loyalty, only ever losing one employee other than to retirement.

The partners' compensation has evolved over time. When Steve joined Charles's practice, Charles was doing about $1.7 million and

Steve as a new advisory was doing less than $100,000. Based on the legacy business they made a decision to split their business 85 percent to Charles and 15 percent to Steve up to $2 million, and then 50/50 on all business above that. As their business grew and the percentages got closer the partners decided to make it a 50/50 even split.

Communication

The team holds a weekly meeting every Monday at 8:00 a.m. One of the client associates puts together an agenda and prints out the calendar of the past week, the current week, and the next week. All the team members compile agenda items they want to discuss during the meeting. The calendar is reviewed, team agenda items are covered, and specific clients are discussed. These meetings typically last thirty to forty-five minutes. The client associates have a weekly meeting that lasts between fifteen and thirty minutes and covers items and issues that relate just to them.

The team also has a year-end planning meeting that covers the next year's planning items, reviewing the playbook, and reviewing the team's clients. Additionally, they have as needed situational "team huddles" that might include a big win, a new issue, or a specific idea that needs to be communicated.

The partners also communicate with the rest of the team after they complete a significant client or prospective client meeting. The partners compare notes and pass information on to the other team members through email with follow-up tasks assigned. The objective is that every team member is aware of what happened during a significant client or prospective client meeting.

Offering and Process

According to Charles "we are not organized around us—we are organized around the client." A core part of their value proposition is their process. Their process starts with the introduction meeting with a prospective client. They focus on the prospect's goals, dreams, objectives, and current holdings. They also discuss what the prospect does for fun and what their passions are, working to build rapport and trust.

If a strong connection is made and the prospect wants to move forward a financial plan is completed. The plan is based on three goals—essential, important, and aspirational. The partners schedule a follow-up meeting with spouses present and walk them through the plan and review the three goals. This meeting also focuses on where the prospective client is now and what the partners believe they can get them to. It's really a concept sale: Reviewing the possibilities and positioning the power of the holistic approach enables the partners to be a family office—designing and implementing the financial plan to reach the client's goals.

Another part of the process is the introduction of the new client to every member of the team. Charles calls this the "Captain Von Trapp Moment." Everyone on the team lines up and spends sixty seconds talking about what they do, where they went to college, and a little bit about their background. The objective is for the new potential client to have a high level of confidence in the team. Lastly, a proposal is built—typically half fee based and half commission based.

The cornerstones of the team's offering are their investment models—portfolio construction, core portfolios, and rebalancing. Intergenerational planning is another strength of the team. Another core of their offering is their service model—monthly contacts, quarterly and annual reviews. Charles and Steve recognize that they need to focus on what's most important to their clients, not what the S&P index does. According to Charles, "When we start talking about their daughter with special needs that's what they want to talk about—it's about their family, not the markets."

According to Steve, one of the team's objectives is to identify two or three very specific goals that aren't performance-related—such as income derived from the portfolios, tax efficient investing, and intergenerational planning. They have crafted a very compelling value proposition that summarizes their offering: "*We are a seven-person team that works with a very select few high net worth families. Normally, it's corporate executives; a retired person or someone who sold a business. We help them with all their wealth management needs from building a custom financial plan to building a custom portfolio or hand-picking individual bonds and securities that are suitable to them. We help our clients develop an estate plan that is consistent with their goals and objectives, educating their kids and providing appropriate lending opportunities.*"

Leadership

The partners want to make sure that everyone on the team is fully up to speed. Charles said, "*We want them to know our strategy, we want them to know our clients, and about the results. We talk about at least one client at every team meeting, choosing one that all the team members might not know very well.*"

The partners send an email to the entire team members each week to update them on their monthly business results. Charles shared one that stated: *Hey gang here's what we produced for this month, up 16 percent over the same month last year and it's the best November we have ever had, fantastic job, lunch on us this week.*

The partners expect the employees to come in with a positive attitude every day, and the partners lead by example with their own positive attitudes. According to Charles, "an employee's attitude is something they have complete control over."

Marketing

The partners are always prospecting—which is based primarily on generating proactive referrals from their clients. For instance, one of their clients is a senior executive of a natural gas company. Charles looked at the company's website, called the client and asked him if he could provide an introduction to the Director of Land, which this client agreed to do. Shortly after meeting him, they were able to convert this prospect and landed a new $11 million client. Charles then asked the same executive about another person listed on the website. The client mentioned that he was a hunter and would hit it off with Charles, who also likes to hunt. This introduction resulted in another $10 million client.

Steve uses the same technique and routinely reviews clients' websites and asks for favorable introductions, which he most often gets. In the past twelve months using this technique they have acquired five new clients with a cumulative asset transfer of $100 million.

JIM AND JIM JR.: A FAMILY PARTNERSHIP

Structure

Jim's team started as a vertical team but has evolved into a horizontal team when his son, Jim Jr., gained the experience to be a senior partner. There are currently four FA team members (Jim, Jim Jr., Ken, and Mary), two senior client associates, and one junior client associate. Jim has 45 percent of the team split, Jim Jr. 35 percent, Ken 10 percent, and Mary 10 percent. The team does $5 million on $1.1 billion in assets and has a total of three hundred relationships.

Roles and Responsibilities

Jim turned over the managing partner role to Jim Jr. three years ago. Jim Jr. handles most of the team issues, does the performance reviews, and tracks the results of the team. The father, as the senior partner, works with his legacy clients who typically have at least $1 million. Jim Jr. has continued to develop client relationships that Jim assigned him and has developed quite a few million+ clients on his own, primarily through his involvement on the board of his college and other nonprofit boards, using the "Right Place—Right People" strategy outlined in "Building a Marketing Division" (Chapter 10).

Ken has been with the team for more than thirty years and works as a relationship manager for a number of the team's smaller relationships, as well as some client relationships that he has brought in on his own. Ken is considered the team authority on the rules and regulations of retirement plans and serves as a team resource in that area. He also takes responsibilities for the team's mortgages and other lending and insurance offerings. While Ken's business generated doesn't equal the 10 percent equity split he receives, they pay him that amount because of the resource he is in his areas of expertise and the problem-solving he is able to help the team with. Ken is self-sufficient and uses very little of the client associate's time. As Jim thinks about Ken's replacement longer term he is looking for someone who would help with asset and relationship management, not necessarily to be an asset gatherer.

Mary was brought onto the team four years ago as part of the team's longer-term succession plan. Jim and Ken anticipate retirement within ten years and the client base is too large for Jim Jr. to handle by himself. Mary brought some clients with her when she joined the team and has been assigned some of Jim and Jim Jr.'s smaller relationships. She also has expertise in larger group retirement plans (401k). I asked Jim why the team brought Mary aboard and he responded, *"We liked her, and that's key to anything on a team. It's like a marriage—you better get along and trust one another. It's evolving really well and I believe it will only get better. As our confidence in her builds, we will share more and more of our existing relationships with her."*

There are three client associates, and each is responsible for one partner's clients. They handle every aspect of the operational and administrative side of those relationships. The client associates support each other when one of them is away from their desks. One of the client associates is in charge of opening new accounts, whether it's a brand-new relationship, an existing client opening another account, or a family member opening a smaller account. All three of the team's client associates are registered.

Accountability—Performance

Jim Jr. does performance reviews on all of the team members twice a year. The reviews include equity split percentages for the partners and reviewing the nonpartner team members' performance of their assigned responsibilities. These are candid conversations to review strengths and areas of development. These reviews go beyond job performance, including attitude, work ethic, and teamwork: Is there a lot of drama associated with their work, are there a lot of absences, are they willing to go above and beyond their assigned responsibilities?

Compensation

The client associates get paid a base salary by the firm and then the team provides a bonus. According to Jim, "We pay our client associates a great deal more than most support people in our market." According to Jim they have never cut their employees' pay, even when they didn't take raises for themselves when the team's business was down. In a typical year, the bonuses the team pays the client associates matches the salary they get if they perform at their jobs at a high level. As an example, if the base salary is $50,000, they would get an additional $50,000 bonus from the team. The bonuses are based on the performance reviews with some subjectivity involved. Each partner contributes to the bonus depending on what their equity split is.

Communication

The core of the team communication is the daily morning huddle. The huddle occurs first thing in the morning and every team member brings lists of items to be covered. Typically, these are administrative or service-related items. They also do a quick run-through of upcoming client reviews and what is needed for these meetings. These daily morning huddles take fifteen minutes.

Jim explained that the mornings are typically busier than afternoons, so the client associates also meet with their assigned partners right after lunch and review any items that need to be covered that have accumulated in the morning.

KEN: A PROCESS-BASED PRACTICE

Structure

Ken runs a vertical team, taking an 86 percent equity split. His junior partner Mike gets 14 percent. Mike is considerably younger than Ken and is an important part of Ken's long-term succession plan. The team is doing $3 million in business, on $330 million in assets. Ken's team has three hundred core client relationships, with 75 percent of them assigned to Ken and 25 percent to Mike.

The team has two senior client associates. The team also has a junior client associate who works part time. Only one of the client associates is registered.

Roles and Responsibilities

Ken is the primary contact for the clients and does the majority of the reviews. Lately, he is assigning more of that responsibility to Mike. Ken is also the rainmaker on the team, being responsible for business development and marketing.

Mike has responsibilities for doing the team's planning work, lending and mortgages, and the day-to-day running of the investment portfolios. He also has responsibilities to interact with all the vendors. The team uses a discretionary platform that consists of eighteen portfolios run for their clients that vary in size and risk. According to Ken they have something for everyone. Mike runs those discretionary portfolios and when he and Ken decide to make changes, it's his job to get them implemented. Ken and Mike have regular investment meetings where they discuss portfolio and asset allocation changes. Mike has limited business development responsibilities.

Ken is a big believer that his two senior client associates are responsible for many of the referrals he gets as the result of the outstanding service they provide his clients. The most senior client associate does all the order entry for the team, submits the annuity orders, implements the team's asset allocations for the annuities, and handles all the new account openings. The other senior client associate does the behind-the-scenes work to support those efforts. Additionally, the other senior associate, while not entering orders, moves money, does journal entries and performs other administrative and operational tasks. Both senior associates divide the administrative responsibilities on an as-needed basis so that they can cover for each other if one person is out sick or on vacation.

There is one part-time team member who works about ten hours a week. She is in charge of sending out Thanksgiving, holiday, and birthday cards as well as providing clients gifts at the holidays. She does all the "copy talk" cut and paste—this is a voice recording system that transfers to the written word—and keeps the client contact system up to date. She also helps support the logistics on the team's events, and supports the other client associates as needed.

Looking forward, Ken is giving strong consideration to adding his son to the team in a business development role. He would like his son to get the CFP designation. He has also identified a young lady that he would like to hire to help Mike with the portfolio management. This woman will be added to the team if she can get a CIMA designation. Ken's goal is to have more professional designations and increased capacity for the team. His vision is that he would bring his son as a new financial advisor under his firm's program and the young lady as an employee, not an equity partner.

Process

Ken's team uses a postcard process for client reviews. The CAs send out postcards to each client that says, "It's time for your quarterly review—please call us to schedule a convenient time" and according to Ken most people do call. The client associates tell them what dates and times are available for either Ken or Mike, just like a doctor's office. Ken does the reviews with the majority of the clients taking an hour for an in-person review, and thirty minutes when it's on the phone.

In Ken's words: "Imagine a doctor's office with seven doors down a hallway and the doctor goes from one room to the next. Someone else has taken the patient's temperature, filled in the chart and asked the symptoms. All the review is prepped and if you have your team doing that behind the scenes it runs incredibly well."

Ken believes in customizing the reviews to the client but at the same time controlling the time. When Ken finishes a review, he writes down what needs to be done in blue ink. The client associates write back to him with black ink and all corrections are done in red. The reason for this color-coded system is so that nothing gets lost in translation or falls through the cracks.

Compensation

The client associates both get a firm base salary and a performance bonus, which is not based on a percentage of the team's production. Over the years, Ken has raised the compensation based on performance and experience, and while he is willing to raise the supplemental compensation he never reduces it.

Ken did not provide me with specific numbers but was clear to point out that his most senior and registered CA is paid significantly more than other client associates because of her loyalty and performance. The other two CAs don't earn as much because they are not registered and haven't been working with the team as long as the most senior CA.

Communication

The primary form of team communication is the weekly meeting. Ken believes these meetings serve as a way of evaluating his team members' performance because he holds the team members accountable for what they are working on, their follow up, team spirit, and can-do attitude. He also believes that consistently holding these meetings is important, even if a team member is on vacation. He feels that an important reason for these meetings are so the client associates can escalate problems or issues they are working on that need his input. The weekly team meeting has a roundtable format and Ken and Mike share what they are working on—their priorities for the week and a review of the upcoming calendar, as well as their prospect pipeline. That is followed by a "round robin" by the other team members of questions, challenges, successes, and concerns. Typically, these weekly team meeting are no longer than thirty minutes and are held Monday mornings.

HENRY AND TOM: SUCCESSION PLANNING

Structure

This is a vertical team with all the business going through Henry's production number and Tom compensated as an employee.

The team formed over twenty years ago when Tom was a new advisor and Henry was asked to mentor him while he was in training. At the end of Tom's training program their philosophies meshed so well that they formed a partnership. Henry brought Tom on his team as a senior investment associate—a fully paid employee. However, as Henry is transitioning into retirement that structure is changing, with Tom becoming a full equity partner and Henry a senior consultant during the transition over to Tom.

They have structured the team in a way that both of them have relationships with the clients, ensuring that the clients are comfortable talking to either one of them. In some cases, a client might gravitate toward one or another but for the most part they are interchangeable. Tom does more of the analytics for the team, monitoring the investment portfolios. Henry is the relationship manager for the majority of the clients and is responsible for business development. They have one senior client associate who has worked with them for over ten years and in Henry's words, "She is unbelievable—well respected by our clients and a real team player."

The team currently works with eighty-five core client relationships and manages $275 million in assets, producing $2 million in business.

Succession Planning

In anticipation of Henry transitioning out of the business the client reviews are being done together. According to Tom, *"What we are trying to do for those clients that Henry has primarily worked with is to put me in the room to build deeper rapport to ensure the transition goes smoothly."*

From Tom's perspective, the succession planning has been a factor for joining Henry's team from the beginning. Over the past twenty years he has been mentored by Henry on building client relationships, developing a deep understanding of the capital markets, and implementing a world-class wealth management process. He also appreciates that although he might have made more money as an equity partner, his long-term reward is taking over the practice. Tom feels totally comfortable with the time investment that he made.

Compensation

While all the business runs through Henry, Tom is paid a salary and a 10 percent bonus on the team's total production. On a $2 million practice, Tom's compensation would be approximately $250,000. The team pays their senior client associate 2 percent of the team's business, which is approximately $40,000 in supplemental compensation.

JOHN: THE MASTER OF SCALE

Structure

John's team is the third-highest producing team with one of the largest financial services firm in the industry. John runs a vertical team with John being the sole equity partner. John has a junior partner, Harry, who is interchangeable with John. John covers half the clients (the most affluent ones) and Harry covers the other half. The team has an investment strategist who is also the relationship manager for several of the team's clients. The team has an analyst who is responsible for portfolio management, and a junior analyst who supports him. They have five client managers who are responsible for servicing assigned clients and two junior client associates that support them. In addition, they have a full-time team manager who is John's chief of staff and handles the day-to-day oversight of the team operations.

John values the loyalty and tenure of his team members. His chief of staff has been with him for twenty-seven years.

Process

The team has a very defined mission regarding whom they choose to serve and how they serve them. In John's words, "*we sell chocolate cake and that's all we sell—but we sell really good chocolate cake.*" John feels like by having a very concise deliverable and finding similar clients, it makes their business very scalable and easy to run.

The team is very disciplined about who they add as a client. John referenced his early days when he had six hundred clients who had fifty different approaches and portfolios. He found this model limited his growth potential, and has since made it more scaleable to reach the business levels the team has now achieved.

John believes it's important to have a limited menu that's repeatable and appeals to their target market. He also provided an example of how the team has scaled their business through their investment process. They run two models or styles of long-term growth and enhanced income. Every client is in some combination of those two models and it's the client manager's job to make sure they know what the models are for each client and to ensure they stay in the models. When new money comes in and out they reallocate appropriately so the models stay consistent. This practice has increased the clients' cash flow over time which resonates with their client base, which is typically first-generation wealth creators who sold their business.

The team has an investment committee that meets once a quarter. The purpose is to make sure their investment models are on track, and evaluate current market conditions, private equity opportunities, and the messaging they want to provide their clients.

Roles and Responsibilities

John describes his responsibilities as 30 percent contacting the team's best clients and 70 percent business development. He is responsible for fifty of the team's largest hundred client relationships and Harry is responsible for the other fifty. He has been working with Harry to assume more responsibility for client contact, so the clients look at him as their primary relationship manager. John still drops in during client reviews that are assigned to Harry and will talk to clients periodically, but it's clear that Harry is their primary contact.

The client managers are each responsible for every aspect of the client relationships that they are assigned to other than the client reviews. They handle all of the service needs of the clients, including preparation of the client reviews, day-to-day contact, and making their clients feel special in every way they can. The client managers also work with their assigned clients' CPAs and attorneys. They do the reallocations following the direction of the team's investment committee.

John provided an example of a client that he did a recent review with. The client manager prepared for the review, John called the client (out of state), and the review took twenty-one minutes. He does four reviews with this client a year. The client manager contacts this client monthly between the reviews to check in. The client generates $200,000 of business a year—so John makes $90,000 a year for eighty minutes of his time, or approximately $70,000 an hour—that's scale.

The two junior client associates help the client managers with administrative or operational overflow. John admits that the team is overstaffed but his view is that he would rather have one more employee to ensure extraordinary service than one less and lower the team's capacity to provide that level of service.

The analyst job is to review and screen investment opportunities and monitor their investment models. She reviews available private equity offerings, overlaying the team's criteria for attractive offerings.

John's vision of the future is a pod system. The pod system is based on having five people that would consist of three senior client managers and two junior client associates. Each pod would be responsible for sixty to seventy-five ultra-high net worth clients. Because the team is adding ten new ultra-high net worth clients a year, John envisions having three pods within three years.

Accountability—Performance

John has an accountability process where he rates the client managers and client associates on a scale of 1 to 5, and their compensation is based on that score. He bases their rating on observations and feedback from other team members and clients. When I asked John how he determined the criteria for each rating he told me the following: "*A 1 is somebody who shows up to work, does what's necessary, and leaves. A 3 is someone who excels at their job, and 5 is an employee that does extraordinary work—giving their job 110 percent.*"

John does a review on every employee twice a year and he feels currently that every team member is either a 4 or a 5.

Compensation

John compensates the client managers and client associates through a base salary and annual raises based on their experience and the team's performance. He typically gives them a 2 to 3 percent raise every year plus an additional bonus based on how the team does. These bonuses are typically a third of the team's growth rate. As an example, if the team growth rate is 10 percent in a given year, a "5" employee would get a 3 percent bonus based on the growth of the business. For example, if the business grew by $1.5 million their individual bonus would be $45,000. If they had a 4 rating it would be a 2 percent bonus. However, if the business drops he never cuts pay; the salaried employee just wouldn't receive the supplemental bonus.

John's senior client managers earn approximately $100,000 a year plus $2,000 for every year they are on the team. A junior associate makes $45,000 to $50,000 and an automatic 15 percent raise annually for the first two years to ensure they are earning $60,000 to $65,000 by the end of the third year if they have done a good job. John has committed 15 to 20 percent of his compensation toward the team compensation. This year it is 19.2 percent.

Leadership

John considers himself as the leader of the team although he delegates much of the day-to-day management of the client managers and client associates to his chief of staff. He believes his most important leadership role is to provide a vision for the team to continue to grow. He also believes that his role is to hire the right people to join the team and inspire them to give their best. John provided several examples of his leadership, "*I have established a policy that every team member gets a free lunch if they are willing to work through lunch. Another team policy is that every team member votes whenever we are considering bringing on a new team member. Anyone can blackball a hire—it takes a 100 percent vote to bring on a new hire.*"

NELSON: THE RELATIONSHIP MANAGER ROLE

Structure

Nelson runs a vertical team with two other partners. Nelson gets 80 percent of the business and each of the other partners get 10 percent based on the legacy business to which they contributed. However, beyond the legacy business the team established a single pool split for new business the other partners bring in that is 70 percent to them and 30 percent to Nelson. The 30 percent to Nelson is to pay for the investment process he developed and the administrative support he provides, including a relationship manager to work with their smaller clients.

Nelson looks at his team as a franchise opportunity and has encouraged other financial advisors to join under the 70/30 split arrangement. In addition to the three core partners the team has added five other partners that fit the franchise model. These five franchise partners join the team at an 85/15 split (85 percent them and 15 percent to the team) and then split the new business at 70/30 (70 percent them and 30 percent to the team).

The benefits to the franchise team members are a well-defined investment model that includes four discretionary strategies that are managed with different risk-adjusted matrices. The team also has designed a world-class pitch book that has been very effective in communicating the value of their team. The franchise team members have the benefit of being part of a team with $1.6 billion in assets that's ranked by *Barron's* and *Fortune* as one of the top financial advisory teams. They also get access to the team's relationship managers, and a high-quality service model to provide their clients. These franchise partners can focus on bringing in new clients and assets with everything else being taken care of.

The team has four relationship managers, five administrative managers, and two wealth management strategists. There is also an executive assistant who doubles as the team's operations manager, keeping track of expenses, team organization, and client events.

Nelson's core team manages $840 million in assets and does $7.3 million with a total of eight hundred relationships. The extended team, which includes the franchise team partners, will produce $15 million on $1.6 billion in assets.

Accountability—Performance

Nelson is the managing director of the team. He manages all staff decisions and does the staff reviews. He meets with every team member and has a performance review with all the client associates and wealth management associates. In preparation for the reviews he gets feedback from the partners they support and other team members that work with them. Each review lasts thirty minutes and in addition to reviewing their performance he asks the following questions:

- *"Are you happy with your job?"*
- *"Is there anything you wish you didn't have to do?"*
- *"Is there anything that you would want to do more of?"*
- *"Is there anything I can do to help your job and help you be more productive?"*
- *"Is there anything you want to share with me that you think I need to know?"*

Nelson also does quarterly reviews with the team's relationship managers. He focuses on their activity level, specifically frequency of contact with their assigned clients. He reviews their sales force data, emails, and phone call logs to determine how many contacts they are making. On average, each relationship manager makes five hundred contacts per quarter. Nelson can quickly see if one is doing more or less than the average.

Roles and Responsibilities

There are four positions on the team: financial advisor (partners), relationship managers, wealth management strategists, and administrative assistants. The following is a description of each:

Relationship Manager (RM). This is a nonproducing team member who is paid a salary and a bonus that is a small percentage of the team's production. Their job is to call the client every month and maintain the relationship. During the monthly contact they review client asset allocation and share the team's current view of the markets and what the client's last twelve months rolling performance for her accounts is, as well as making personal connections whenever possible. The RMs participate in every face-to-face meeting and attend every seminar or luncheon for their assigned clients. According to Nelson, "the RMs are always involved with their assigned clients. They are like a dental hygienist for a dentist, or a nurse for a doctor—they are always present."

The financial advisor assigned to the client comes and goes when needed to give advice, adding a layer of competency necessary to guide the relationship in all aspects of the client's goals. The goal is for each relationship manager to cover 150 client relationships, but that can be stretched to 175 and in some cases up to 190.

The FA meets with each of the clients they have assigned to the relationship manager at least once a year. These annual reviews typically take an hour and each FA will cover approximately 150 clients. The FAs block two or three days a month for these reviews and can hold up to six in a day. The wealth management strategist prepares all the reviews in advance. As a result of this process each client is contacted monthly by an RM (except the smallest clients, which are typically quarterly) and annually by the FA, whom they also have access to if needed.

Nelson has a dozen clients who have over $10 million for which he is the relationship manager and does all the contacts himself. Nelson's clients that his relationship manager covers have on average $5 million. The team does not have a hard and fast minimum but the majority of their clients' relationships have over a million dollars to invest. The relationship managers have a wide range of previous experience: a law firm recruiter, a PR firm employee, and a development officer from a private school.

Wealth Management Strategist. This is a nonproducing team member. Their job is to work with the relationship manager and the financial advisor to build the client review kits, to look at their financial plans, and prepare the Monte Carlo simulations tool to projected future income stream scenarios and risk to the portfolios as well as all the other goals associated with the client. They also prepare pitch books for prospective clients and schedule meetings. They work in the background to make sure the client meetings and all of the presentation materials are available for the relationship managers and financial advisors.

Administrative Assistant. This job focuses on "sensitive issues with money" that include transferring money, and onboarding new accounts. This position deals with all the paperwork to support the structure of the account system. The administrative assistant talks to their assigned clients frequently. Each client knows who her designated administrative assistant is and will call him with any operational issue or question.

The team operates in pods that consist of client associates, relationship managers, and wealth management specialists. Each pod handles four financial advisors and there are two pods that support the team. The pods communicate with each other and when needed can support each other.

Compensation

Nelson is committed to paying 15 percent of the team's compensation to nonproducing team members. The nonproducing team members are paid a bonus based on a percentage of gross production. It's paid monthly throughout the year based on the production generated. The team pays an entry-level administrative manager or wealth management specialist $35,000 to $50,000. After two years and once they become registered they would move up to the $50,000 to $75,000 range. After five years if they are registered and doing a fantastic job they could make up to $100,000.

The average compensation range for a wealth management specialist is $45,000 to $50,000. The typical starting salary for a relationship manager is $70,000 to $75,000 a year depending on past background. After five years it's not uncommon for them to make $100,000 with a salary capped at $110,000 with small raises. If a relationship manager wants to make more than the cap they have to become a financial advisor, which requires them to be capable of adding million+ clients to the team. According to Nelson: "I've always thought that compensation—if you paid a little bit more than average and you get someone that's a little better than average then the quality of work that they are going to produce is significantly better than average. So, for a little bit more, you get a whole lot more productivity."

Communication

The team holds four meetings a month. The team meets every Monday morning at 8:45. The meeting is mandatory and it lasts for forty minutes. The team has an agenda and every team member covers an assigned agenda item. Nelson's goal is to get as many people as possible to speak during the meeting. One team member may review the ninety-day calendar that includes vacations, team events, and holidays. Another team member will cover the highlights of economic information, strategic updates, and revisions from their firm.

Another team member might cover the bond markets. Someone else covers updates on international markets. Another team member will review new business, new clients, and provide a business update. Another team member will highlight an investment idea or a theme they are going to work on that month outside of their fee-based accounts. Another team member will report on all bonds that are maturing, new cash available, or high cash balances. They also have a team member who gives an update on mortgage rate and lending rates. Nelson sums up the main points and themes of the meeting.

Nelson is committed to keeping the meeting to forty minutes and is responsible for keeping the meeting on track. If someone gets off track or gets long-winded Nelson cuts them off and in a nice way gets them back on topic. According to Nelson, "*after you do that for a few months, everyone gets it, when the meeting starts everyone knows it's all business.*"

The team also holds a monthly financial advisor meeting that is just for the partners. The focus of this meeting is to decide what projects they are going to work on. There is a need for uniformity because they want the relationship managers to have a singular message. The FA meeting is designed to develop a unified strategy and message so the rest of the team understands the strategy and has unified talking points. In addition Nelson shares other issues with the partners about what's happening on the team and other relevant updates.

Nelson holds a monthly relationship manager meeting so that he can get feedback from them about what's happening with their clients. He also checks in with them about their interaction with the administrative staff and the partners as well as what they are going to market for that month.

Nelson also holds a monthly department head meeting that includes one partner, one relationship manager, and one administrative manager. At that meeting they discuss communication and workflow issues, keeping the team productive, and how to be better organized. These meeting are all typically forty minutes long.

Hiring

Nelson has sole responsibility for hiring new team members and it's not unusual for him to interview as many as ten people for a job. He also includes multiple team members in the hiring process. He requires a unanimous decision before an offer is made. Nelson believes the quality of hiring is essential to the team's high functioning. He wants to hire leaders that are ambitious. The following are the sources that he uses for hiring:

- **Team members.** Do you know anyone who is frustrated in their current job or do you have a family member that would fit in with the team?
- **Office.** Nelson notifies the office he works in that he has a team opening.
- **Advertising.** Nelson advertises in local newspapers and online for potential team members, posting job descriptions for specific positions.

Vision

Every year Nelson goes through what he describes as a "creative destruction process—taking the practice apart and putting it back together working toward continuous improvement." He considers this process a constant course correction. The following are the areas that Nelson looks at during his annual creative destruction process:
- What's changing?
- What's different?
- What's new?
- What we are doing that is still appropriate?
- What do we need to change?
- What are we going to do differently?

PAUL: **THE LAW FIRM MODEL**

Structure

Paul believes that the structure of a law firm fits very well with a financial services practice and has organized his team using that structure. The team has a hierarchy of senior partners, junior partners, client relationship managers, and client associates.

This team is a horizontal model with two senior partners who are the partners with the "name on the door," Paul and Jerry. Paul gets 75 percent of the equity split and Jerry gets 25 percent. They have five relationship managers (this is a different job description than Nelson's RM role) who have different roles on the team including planning, investment management, and business development. Currently the team does not have any junior partners who are financial advisors "but don't have their name on the door." To move from being a junior partner to a senior partner you have to generate $1 million or more in business. To become a junior partner, you have to be in the top 40 percent of advisors with the same level of experience in the business. Typically, a junior partner does between $400,000 and $1,000,000 in business. There are three client associates responsible for client service.

The team does $4.5 million in business and manage $620 million in assets. That encompasses 170 households with $1 million+ assets and a total of 700 total client relationships. The team has grown from $650,000 to $4.5 million since Paul joined the team in 2002.

Roles and Responsibilities

The relationship manager role came from Paul's observation of many people in his office who were not succeeding as financial advisors but were talented and good at other aspects of the job such as investment management, planning, and business development. Paul approached these individuals who were financial advisors and offered them jobs on his team as salaried team employees in RM roles that leveraged their expertise. He offered these employees the opportunity to become a junior partner if they reach a compensation level of $150,000 salary and bonus (the equivalent of $400,000 in production).

As a senior partner, Paul works with the majority of the $1 million+ clients and all the $10 million+ clients. Jerry is also a senior partner and works with some million+ and some smaller but high-potential clients. Paul and Jerry work together on the team's strategy, deal with human resources issues, work with the team's largest clients, and set the investment strategy and policy. Paul believes that to be a successful senior partner you have to have four essential traits: understand investments, planning skills, business development skills, and the ability to build strong relationships with clients and prospects.

The team has an analyst who implements the investment strategy at the partners' direction.

The relationship managers back up on the senior partners' client relationships. They create and implement the financial plans. They follow the investment committee's three model portfolios and match the appropriate portfolios with their clients. The investment committee consists of the two senior partners and the team's analyst.

The business development RM is focused on bringing in new clients and assets. He has good impact, outstanding interpersonal skills, and is an excellent golfer. He has had good success in introducing affluent prospects to the team. If the prospect is over a million he typically refers these new relationships to Jerry since Paul is at capacity. If the prospect is under a million he will refer them to another RM. He stays involved with the new client and the assigned relationship manager until the client is comfortable. He spends the majority of his time outside the office meeting and entertaining prospective clients.

Compensation

The team has a single pool number for everyone. Each team member gets some percentage of that pool as the majority of their compensation. Paul explains the rationale for one pool: "*On our team we have a single pool number so that everyone's interested in the success of their peers. If your peer is having a good day, it means you are having a good day—because everyone on the team is paid on the same pool number. We're capitalists with a socialist flair.*"

RMs typically make between $100,000 and $120,000 with 80 percent of their compensation based on the team's business. The RMs also have the opportunity to earn a bonus, which is typically $12,000. The bonus is not easy to achieve and is entirely objective. As an example, for the business development RM: 10 basis points (one tenth of a percent) on every million of new assets brought in as long as it's at least $5 million.

Paul's logic is that he puts talented people in roles they are good at and then he gives them incentives to excel. If an RM achieves $150,000 in compensation they become a junior partner and their entire compensation is based on their equity split. To clarify, $150,000 in compensation translates to $400,000 in production, which is 10 percent of the team's current production of $4 million. The new junior partner would keep the 10 percent split forever. If the new junior partner does an exceptional job of bringing in new assets, the split could be renegotiated at a future date.

Paul and Jerry have a sliding scale split. They split the business 75/25 but split the growth rate 50/50. For example, if the team grows 20 percent in a year, growing from $4.0 million to $4.8 million, Paul and Jerry would split the first 4.0 million 75/25 and the growth of $800,000 50/50—which would change their split to 73/27.

The relationship managers get a small base salary of approximately $25,000 plus 1.7 percent of the team's total production ($75,000, based on $4.5 million) plus a $12,000 bonus based on a specific objective, which provides an approximate total compensation of $100,000 to $120,000.

The following are examples of team bonuses by role:

- Client associates receive $500 for every referral the team receives. Paul believes that extraordinary service drives referrals and this is a way the team can incentivize client associates to provide that level of service.

- Non-business development relationship managers receive a bonus based on the breadth of the relationship, since they are in a planning role with the team's clients. Their firm can measure that metric.

- Business development relationship managers receive 10 basis points for each million brought in as long as the $5 million threshold is met.

Accountability and Performance

Paul and Jerry review team members at the end of each year and allocate compensation. Each team member is also asked about what they did best during the past year, about areas they could improve in, and about what they want out of the next year.

Process

Paul believes that most financial advisors don't delegate well. He believes processes need to be created to get things done and the financial advisor needs to monitor the processes but doesn't need to be involved in every detail of implementing them.

Paul shared his thoughts about the team's processes, "I hate the idea of doing something one time and not creating a process around it." The team has a single growth model, a single income model, and a cash model as the basic investment process.

Communication

The team has three meetings a week:

- **Relationship manager and partners meeting.** This includes everyone but the three client associates and is held on Tuesdays. Past meeting notes are reviewed to make sure everything was executed. They also discuss market updates or changes to their model portfolios.

- **Client associate meeting.** This Wednesday meeting includes the three client associates and its purpose is to keep the client associates on the same page and discuss topics that are relevant to their roles. The RM and partners meeting notes are shared so they can reconcile what they have been delegated to what has been done. They are also able to help each other with issues and challenges. They reconcile their task lists and come up with ideas of how to streamline administrative processes and improve communication among team members. They are also looking for ways to improve the overall service experience.

- **Team meeting.** This Thursday meeting includes all team members, and every team member is expected to participate in developing the agenda. This meeting provides a venue to download everything that came from the client associate and RM and partners meetings. This meeting is the only time during the week when the entire team is at the same place at the same time. The team also reviews the next week's calendar. The business development RM updates the team on his activities and reviews the prospect pipeline. Clients are discussed and events that are occurring in their lives are reviewed so everyone on the team has a deeper knowledge of the team's best clients.

Typically, each of the three meetings last an hour—so every team member has to dedicate two hours a week to meetings. The following is an agenda of a typical Thursday team meeting:

- Summary of weekly client reviews (by client name and date)
- Summary of new million+ relationships
- Business development goals and results and notes
- Client reassignments
- Random acts of kindness
- Upcoming client events
- Clients' kids we need to know better
- Team administrative issues
- Lending rates
- Tax, financial planning, and investment updates
- Who and what are we forgetting?
- Who updated this agenda—note: there is peer pressure for all team members to contribute to the agenda

A FINAL NOTE

The wealth management business has evolved in so many positive ways since I started as a Merrill Lynch financial advisor in 1980. As I reflect on the past thirty-eight years, I believe one of the most significant and positive changes has been the evolution from financial advisors that were solo practitioners to financial advisory teams.

It is my hope that after reading this book and implementing the team best practices, that you will lead your team and reap all the rewards of being part of a highly functioning team.

Appendix A

The Team Best Practices Checklist

If you already have a team in place, you can see at what level your team is functioning. Does your team incorporate these best practices at a low, average, or high level? If you are not incorporating these guidelines yet, you are at a low level. If you are doing some of the guidelines, rate yourself as average. If you are incorporating all of them into your existing practice, give yourself a high score.

PROFESSIONAL VALUES

- ❑ Do potential team partners have common values and goals?
- ❑ Do potential team members have a similar work ethic?
- ❑ Do potential team members like and trust each other?
- ❑ Are potential team members committed to investing back into the practice?
- ❑ Are the potential team members aligned on an agreed upon wealth management process?

TEAM STRUCTURE AND FORMATION

- ❑ Determine the best team structure: vertical, horizontal, holistic, alliance.
- ❑ Team members align on an agreed-upon wealth management process.
- ❑ Establish a formal partnership agreement with a dissolution process.
- ❑ Implement an annual review process of partnership agreement and dissolution process.

- ❑ Arrange phone coverage and develop scripts for answering the phone.
- ❑ Set office hours.
- ❑ Implement a dress code.
- ❑ Decide on physical location, office space configuration, and office appearance.
- ❑ Send out a client announcement introducing each team member and their roles and responsibilities.

TEAM VISION

- ❑ Develop a long-term team vision.
- ❑ Create a three-to-five-year business plan to implement your vision.
- ❑ Develop business plan action steps, prioritize them, and assign responsibility.
- ❑ Measure and communicate business plan results monthly.
- ❑ Develop a formal succession plan.
- ❑ Make sure all team members are aware of the succession plan.

ROLES AND RESPONSIBILITIES

- ❑ Determine what skills each partner brings to the team and whether those skills are being optimized.
- ❑ Create an ideal team organizational chart.
- ❑ Assign three to five controllable high-priority goals and activities to each team member.
- ❑ Build a team so that FAs can focus on $500/hour work.
- ❑ Establish clearly defined roles and responsibilities.
- ❑ Organize the team and assign roles and responsibilities.
- ❑ Consider adding an RM role if each FA team member has more than fifty core relationships.
- ❑ Provide a written job description and goals for each team member.
- ❑ Establish a controller role to measure performance.

PERFORMANCE

- ❑ Develop a semiannual review template.
- ❑ Do semiannual reviews with each team member.
- ❑ Focus on fewer (four or five) rather than too many goals for compensation.
- ❑ Set high-priority goals for each team member that define the difference between unacceptable, acceptable, and excellent levels of performance.
- ❑ Take each job description and assign how performance can be measured in activities and results (if appropriate).

COMMUNICATION

- ❑ Conduct weekly team meetings.
- ❑ Conduct semiannual offsite strategic meetings.
- ❑ Conduct daily stand-up meetings.
- ❑ Create agenda templates for weekly and semiannual meetings.
- ❑ Take notes at weekly meetings and distribute them to other team members.

COMPENSATION

- ❑ Compensation should focus on activities and controllable results. It should be based on ratings for each performance goal.
- ❑ Be generous on compensation for loyal high performers.
- ❑ Team compensation range is typically between 7.5 and 15 percent of FA compensation.
- ❑ Establish a bonus pool that all employees participate in if the team reaches or exceeds its goals.
- ❑ Create an annual partnership compensation review meeting to update splits, pools, and succession plan.
- ❑ Recognize outstanding work by individual team members.
- ❑ Develop a compensation budget.
- ❑ Create a team budget that includes business development expenses.

HIRING

- ❏ Review team organization chart to determine duplications and needed additions.
- ❏ Determine budget needed to add team members and make sure all partners are committed to that budget.
- ❏ Develop an organized process for sourcing, hiring, and training new team members.
- ❏ Create a ninety-day probationary period to evaluate performance and attitude.
- ❏ Have partners list their non-big three ($500/hour) activities to create a new job description.

TEAM OFFERING

- ❏ Provide a world-class offering and be able to articulate that offering through a value proposition.
- ❏ Determine the ideal wealth management process that all FA partners are committed to implementing.
- ❏ Determine how model portfolios, asset allocation, and rebalancing will be implemented, monitored, and adjusted.
- ❏ Establish an investment committee.
- ❏ Determine your ideal client.

MARKETING

- ❏ Develop the missionary mindset among all team members.
- ❏ Commit to at least an hour a day of implementing some combination of the seven acquisition strategies.
- ❏ Have a team marketing meeting.
- ❏ Implement a consistent, proactive client referral strategy.
- ❏ Develop a professional referral network.
- ❏ Implement a 10 x 10 event marketing process.
- ❏ Implement the "Right Place—Right People" strategy.
- ❏ Commit to a niche market and develop a niche market plan.

- ❏ Implement the four-part asset away strategy.
- ❏ Build the team's prospect pipeline to fifty qualified candidates and follow a process for managing the pipeline.

PROCESSES

- ❏ Determine ideal new team processes.
- ❏ Evaluate existing processes and FA practices.
- ❏ Periodically review and evaluate all team processes and improve when needed.
- ❏ Assign responsibilities for a team member to develop or update each process, and a timeline for that task.

LEADERSHIP

- ❏ Select a team leader.
- ❏ Assign responsibilities for the team leader.
- ❏ Implement the seven leadership principles into the team.
- ❏ Decide compensation for the team leader.

Appendix B

PROCESS GAP ANALYSIS FORMS

MARKETING DIVISION	Current Rating	Target Rating	Responsibility Name	Completion Date
PROCESS:				
Referrals				
Professional Referral Network				
Event Marketing				
Right Place/Right People				
Assets Held Away				
Prospect Pipeline				
Pitch Book				
Prospect Proposals				
Value Proposition				
Marketing Meeting				
Niche Marketing				

SERVICE DIVISION	Current Rating	Target Rating	Responsibility Name	Completion Date
PROCESS:				
Client Contact				
Documentation				
Personal Stakeholder Touches				
On Boarding				
Client Profile				
Incoming Call Response				
Problem Resolution				
Proactive Service Call				
Client Segmentation				

THE OFFERING/ PRODUCT DIVISION	Current Rating	Target Rating	Responsibility Name	Completion Date
PROCESS:				
Goal-Based Investing				
Wallet Expansion				
Discovery				
Client Reviews				
Investment Discipline				

HUMAN RESOURCES DIVISION	Current Rating	Target Rating	Responsibility Name	Completion Date
PROCESS				
Team Meetings				
Compensation				
Written Job Descriptions				
Hiring				
Performance Reviews				

Index

Index